# Dramatic Monologues

# DRAMATIC MONOLOGUES

## A CONTEMPORARY ANTHOLOGY

Edited by
Samuel Maio

University of Evansville Press
Evansville, Indiana

The text of this book is composed in Times New Roman.
Composition by R.G.
Manufacturing by Thomson-Shore.
Book and Cover Design: W.B. & R.G.

Library of Congress Cataloging-in-Publication Data

Dramatic monologues : a contemporary anthology / [edited] by Samuel Maio. -- 1st ed.
    p. cm.
  ISBN-13: 978-0-930982-67-6
  ISBN-10: 0-930982-67-3
  1. American poetry--20th century. 2. Dramatic monologues. 3. American poetry--21st
century. I. Maio, Samuel, 1955-
  PS615.D74 2008
  821'.0208--dc22

                                                        2008052135


Cover illustration by Jean-Honoré Fragonard, *A Young Girl Reading*, reproduced
by permission of the National Gallery of Art, Washington, D.C.


Acknowledgments and copyright notice for individual poems begin on page 265.

The University of Evansville Press
1800 Lincoln Avenue
Evansville, IN 47722
(812) 488-2963

*For Kathy, mi'amata*

# CONTENTS

"[T]he objective poet, in his appeal to the aggregate human mind, chooses to deal with the doings of man, the result of which dealing . . . is what we call dramatic poetry . . ."

— Robert Browning

# Introduction

From Homer to Virgil, Dante to Milton, Wordsworth to Eliot, and down to the present day, poets have found the dramatic monologue to be useful and effective, an aesthetic favorite proving to enrapture audiences. But what exactly is it? Merely a preferred rhetorical device? An efficacious poetic form of exclusive properties? While many poets and philosophers, ancient and modern, have defined the dramatic monologue with certitude — and many more have assigned to it definitive strictures — few agree on anything but the art's most basic features. Of the three principal genres of poetry — narrative, dramatic, and lyric — the dramatic is perhaps the most difficult to distinguish from the other two, for its essential characteristics of 1) a clearly identifiable speaker or speakers; 2) some thread of story, scene, or situation, however directly or obliquely suggested; and 3) an intense, often personal evocation of emotion, can be found in narrative and lyric poetry as well. This is especially true of the dramatic monologue, which, in resisting general classification, is unique among all types of poetry.

While certain forms of verse lend themselves readily to one genre or another — the ballad to the narrative, for example, and the ballade to the lyric — the dramatic monologue defies such formal correlation simply because any set narrative or lyric form can accommodate it. Keats's ballad "*La Belle Dame sans Merci*" may be considered a dramatic monologue, the final nine stanzas (of the poem's total of twelve) devoted to the knight's self-assessment of his devastation in reply to being asked why he is "Alone and palely loitering." Similarly, François Villon's chilling "Ballade of the Hanged" is a dramatic monologue spoken in the collective voice of the condemned, its envoy a prayer to God for mercy — and in concept any prayer itself is a dramatic monologue, a fine example in the present volume being "San Francesco d'Assisi: Canticle of Created Things," Henry Taylor's verse rendering of an actual 16th-century devout supplication by St. Francis, reminiscent in tone, manner, and content of many Davidic psalms. Richard Wilbur's ballad "The Ride" and Len Krisak's "Ballade: 1985," also in the pages that follow, provide excellent contemporary examples of each form's use in conveying a dramatic monologue.

In contrast to such dynamics of dramatic verse, the confines of the sonnet, say, or the restrictions imposed by the villanelle — two typical lyric modes — prove severely challenging to the poet attempting to use either to convey a narrative. Yet both the sonnet and the villanelle have been used extensively to express dramatic monologues, such as Jonathan Galassi's heartfelt "Siren," one of numerous sonnets represented in the ensuing pages, and Joseph S. Salemi's haunting villanelle "Penelope's Postscript." Often, a particular form can be defined by its structure, meter, and pattern of rhyme, such as the English sonnet's being identified by its fourteen lines of iambic pentameter organized into three quatrains and a couplet, rhyming *ababcdcdefefgg*. However, just as the use of the hymnal stanza in common measure — or the "fourteener" rhythm and rhyme pattern of a quatrain — does not in itself define a ballad, no meter or rhyme scheme can identify a poem as a dramatic monologue, which has proven from the outset to be adaptive and resilient.

The dramatic monologue has appeared through the ages in many different manifestations, from God's directives to Noah, Abraham, Jacob, and Moses and Eliphaz's, Bildad's, and Zophar's speeches to Job as well as Job's replies — to cite but a few of countless examples from the Old Testament alone — to Hamlet's, Othello's, Lear's, and Macbeth's moving epiphanic monologues in Shakespeare's greatest tragedies, through the many instances in Robert Browning, from whom most contemporary practitioners of the art are directly descended, some by way of Ezra Pound. The present volume of *Dramatic Monologues: A Contemporary Anthology* is composed of sonnets, blank verse, and lyric modes of many types. Fluid, the dramatic monologue takes any form necessary, shaping itself to the personality of voice and subject matter it conveys, so it cannot be defined by any single prescription of organizational structure, stanzaic pattern, or metrical rhythm. Rather, it represents — precisely because of the void of any prescribed configuration — a true melding of content and form.

In the absence of any formal definition, then, we must look to the dramatic monologue's constituent aesthetic as well as rhetorical properties. The esteemed literary critic Northrop Frye has provided a useful starting point by defining the dramatic monologue simply as "a monologue in verse" — monologue (from Greek for "one's word") being the central characteristic, just one person speaking with no interlocution, although occasionally the first-person speaker takes the plural form as the collective "we." A soliloquy (from *solus*, Latin for "speaking alone") — such as Jim Barnes's "Under the Tent," Ray Bradbury's "Byzantium I Come Not From," Richard Wilbur's "Peter," and Gail White's "Queen Gertrude's Soliloquy" — is by definition a monologue, the speaker either talking to himself or herself, such as the case in the Wilbur and White poems, which make use of the traditional persona, or the speaker revealing his or her personal thoughts to an audience, as the Barnes and Bradbury poems seemingly do.

In addition to the concept of the monologue, Frye's carefully worded definition emphasizes "verse" as well — that is, poetry adhering to the fundamental and tradition-rich tenets of meter and rhyme. Meter, of course, is the basis of rhythm, the bass-like steady beat underlying every other sound the poem makes and subtly effecting its memorability. Together with its complement of rhyme, meter strengthens and elevates the speaking voice of the dramatic monologue. As Oscar Wilde rhapsodized while writing about Robert Browning's poems, "Rhyme, that exquisite echo which in the Muse's hollow hill creates and answers its own voice; rhyme, which in the hands of a real artist becomes not merely a material element of metrical beauty, but a spiritual element of thought and passion also, waking a new mood, it may be, or stirring a fresh train of ideas, or opening by mere sweetness and suggestion of sound some golden door at which the Imagination itself had knocked in vain; rhyme, which can turn man's utterance to the speech of gods; rhyme, the one chord we have added to the Greek lyre...." This passage exemplifies Wilde's flourishing prose style, yes, yet his claims for the resonating power of rhyme are not *mere* rhetoric, as Gwendolyn Brooks's "We Real Cool," Charles Martin's "Neither Here Nor There," Joshua Mehigan's "Merrily," William Jay Smith's "Death of a Jazz Musician," and Derek Walcott's "A Far Cry from Africa" — among many other poems in *Dramatic Monologues* — so beautifully illustrate by using the music of rhyme to heighten the effects of the representation of thought and emotion. While all of the poems in the present anthology are metrical (a principal condition for inclusion), most are rhymed. The deft use of rhyme, as found in the opening poem, Dick Allen's "On the New Haven Line," and the last, Greg Williamson's "Up in the Air," gives us immense sonic pleasure and stirs our imaginations — as is true of many poems in between, such as Jim Barnes's artfully hidden rhymes in "The Sawdust War," and the clever rhymes in Joyce Carol Oates's "O Crayola!" and John Updike's "Thoughts While Driving Home," both poets validating Wilde's suggestion that rhyme is "a spiritual element of thought and passion."

Yet having addressed the terms "monologue" and "verse" both, what about *drama*? Just what constitutes the *dramatic* in a dramatic monologue? Robert Browning, in his introductory essay to the *Letters of Percy Bysshe Shelley* (1852), distinguishes between two kinds of dramatic verse, the "objective" and the "subjective." The objective poet's "endeavor," Browning writes, "has been to reproduce things external." This type of poet is "the fashioner; and the thing fashioned, his poetry, will of necessity be substantive, projected from himself and distinct." Browning then cites Shakespeare's *Othello* as the primary example of objective dramatic verse. Although Shakespeare based his play on the Italian novella by Giraldi Cinthio, he created Othello's distinctive idiom, giving voice to the character's innermost concerns, which is the essential aim of the objective poet.

The subjective poet, however, does not look externally but internally; a character is not created nor a persona used, but a speaking voice seemingly aligned with the poet's own. Here is Browning at some length on the subjective poet, who

> is impelled to embody the thing he perceives, not so
> much with reference to the many below as to the One
> above him, the supreme Intelligence which apprehends
> all things in their absolute truth — an ultimate view ever
> aspired to, if but partially attained, by the poet's own
> soul. Not what man sees, but what God sees — the *Ideas*
> of Plato, seeds of creations lying burningly on the Divine
> hand — it is toward these that he struggles. Not with the
> combination of humanity in action, but with the primal
> elements of humanity he has to do; and he digs where
> he stands — preferring to seek them in his own soul as
> the nearest reflex of that absolute Mind, according to the
> intuitions of which he desires to perceive and speak. [...]
> He is rather a seer, accordingly, than a fashioner, and
> what he produces will be less a work than an effluence.
> That effluence cannot be easily considered in abstraction
> from his personality — being indeed the very radiance
> and aroma of his personality, projected from it but not
> separated.

Browning essentially suggests that the objective dramatic monologue can be characterized as "exterior," one whose speaker is clearly a persona — such as Othello — and dealing with some external drama usually in the form of narrative. The subjective is "interior," the speaker more closely identified with the poet, whose voice is not "easily considered in abstraction from his personality" and not that of a created character or persona. The interior type of dramatic monologue is introspective, perhaps contemplative of spiritual matters, the speaker "whose study," Browning writes, "has been himself, appealing through himself to the absolute Divine mind," a speaker often engaged in the great metaphysical questions of existence, engaged in self-inquiry aspiring to an epiphany of self-definition.

Because Browning showed a distinct preference for objective verse, as outlined above, it has become axiomatic for many poets and critics to regard the dramatic monologue only through the restrictive criteria of the exterior mode — the use of a persona and reliance on narrative — and so there persists an assumption that the dramatic monologue has declined markedly in use since Browning's time. However, much personal or so-called "confessional" poetry — prevalent during this past half-century — has been written as dramatic monologues of the interior type, a fact obscured by the prevailing academic debate over the authenticity of voice in this kind of poetry and by its subjectivity being considered generally as lyric, not dramatic. Robert Lowell's well-known poems from *Life Studies* — such as "Waking in the Blue," "Memories of West Street and Lepke," and "Skunk Hour" — come readily to mind, as do W. D. Snodgrass's "Heart's Needle" and "April Inventory," the latter included in this volume. R. S. Gwynn's "The Drive-In," Rachel Hadas's "Last Trip to Greece," A. M. Juster's "How We Got to Elmira," X. J. Kennedy's "One-Night Homecoming," David Mason's "*Agnostos Topos*," Henry Taylor's "Goodbye to the Old Friends," Frederick Turner's "At the Casa Paredes," and John Updike's "Dry Spell" are but a partial listing of interior poems, seemingly autobiographically-based, included in *Dramatic Monologues*.

Having discussed the issue of form, parsed Frye's definition "a monologue in verse" by considering the types of voice and kinds of monologue, and having established the concept of verse in terms of the time-honored means of meter and rhyme, all that is left to define is *drama*. Browning's poetry, which spanned the heart of the 19th century and which both Wilde and Swinburne regarded as fiction, competed for the attention of readers during a time when some of the greatest of all novels were written: Emily Brontë's *Wuthering Heights* and sister Charlotte's *Jane Eyre* were both published in 1847, Thackeray's *Vanity Fair* a year later, and Dickens's *David Copperfield* a year after that, serialized from 1849 to 1850 — to list but few during Browning's first phase when he wrote such poems as "Sordello" and "My Last Duchess" — and novels by George Eliot, Anthony Trollope, and many more by Dickens appeared during Browning's major phase (1855-1870), which included such signature poems as "Fra Lippo

Lippi" and " 'Childe Roland to the Dark Tower Came.' " Of course it is only speculative to suggest that his aesthetic practices may have been influenced by the rise of the English novel, but clearly the best of his monologues, in gravitating toward the dramatic narrative and the exterior voice, reflect the most compelling characteristics of the novels of the era.

Drama is the literary representation of conflict — the conflict between reason and will, for example, as illustrated by Anthony Hecht's masterful "The End of the Weekend," with the speaker's struggling against his carnal desire, or it may be "the human heart in conflict with itself," William Faulkner's appropriate phrase from his Nobel address, the emotional or spiritual conflict manifest in any number of differing ways in such poems as Jonathan Galassi's reflective "Turning Forty," Robert Mezey's cool "A Note She Might Have Left" and his elegiac "After Ten Years," Timothy Steele's revelatory "Joseph" and sympathetic "Practice," and Felix Stefanile's angry "Taking Sides with John Ciardi." Conflict, too, can be represented quite literally, such as the violent confrontation depicted in Derek Walcott's "Fight with the Crew" (from *The Schooner* Flight), the domestic violence described in R. S. Gwynn's "Cléante to Elmire," and the horror of war seen in Jim Barnes's "MIA" (from *Bombardier*), Howard Nemerov's "World Lines," and Felix Stefanile's "The Dance at St. Gabriel's." Drama, further, is inherent to Greek literature, which is replete with conflicts arising from clashing with fate and mortals' defiance of the gods — memorably recast, and sometimes reinvented, in the poetry of classicists Anthony Lombardy, David Middleton, and A. E. Stallings, who show us, in their learned and arresting poetry, the immediacy of the ancient myths and lessons. Given the dramatic and metrical emphases of this anthology, it is hardly surprising that many of the contributors have extensive training in classics. A partial listing, in addition to the three poets named above, includes Charles Martin, who has translated definitive editions of Catullus and Ovid, A. M. Juster and Len Krisak, each recently having translated a collection of Horace, and Robert Mezey and Joseph S. Salemi, both noted translators of Latin.

Meter, rhyme, voice, and drama — all are in abundance in the following poems, which include those written by many of the best poets of our time, except for one notable absence. The laws governing the National Endowment for the Arts, which under its "Access to Artistic Excellence" program awarded a grant to the University of Evansville Press to assist the publication of this book, forbid the inclusion of Dana Gioia, whose poems "In Chandler Country," "Planting a Sequoia," "Counting the Children," and "Summer Storm" rank among the finest of contemporary dramatic monologues and certainly would have appeared in the following pages if he were not that agency's Chairman. In an essay published in *The Formalist* in 2002, I make the case that dramatic monologues — and the poems cited above in particular — are central to Gioia's work.

Finally, I would like to take this opportunity to express my appreciation to the staff of the University of Evansville Press, particularly to Rob Griffith who, as a poet, brought special sensibility and care to the manuscript copy of *Dramatic Monologues*, and my foremost gratitude to the Press's Director, William Baer, whose distinguished talents as both a poet and translator often overshadow his important and ongoing achievements as an editor. It is my sincere hope that readers will find in the ensuing pages a few poems that will impress and inspire them, and — as Philip Larkin wrote in his insightful essay "The Pleasure Principle" — bring delight to their lives, just as the many memorable dramatic monologues in this book have enriched my life with immense and continuing pleasure.

— Samuel Maio

**DICK ALLEN**

# *On the New Haven Line*

This is the day you might have died
And never heard a newsboy's cry again,
Or looked out from the window of your train.
This is the day you might have died.

This is the day news might have flown
By letter, telegraph, or telephone,
To friends from Stony Brook to Riverside.
This is the day you might have died.

This is the day you might decide
To visit Croaton Heights or Sally's Lane.
Because, today, you might have died,
No matter what you lose, you gain.

This is the day you might have died
From natural causes, accident, or suicide:
No more adventures in the great unknown
Of hollyhocks and knucklebone.

This is the day. You might have died
And never seen Rowayton in the rain
Or morning glories bloom in Darien.
This is the day you might have died.

## DICK ALLEN

# *William Rimmer:* **Flight and Pursuit**

I saw two men in flight and in pursuit,
Stone castle walls around them and their bodies bent
As if they were the same. They were not the same
But in the leaning shadows of my dream
First I wore a dagger and a sash —
I fled the Lord's white lash;
Then a curving sword, a hood across my face —
I sped through darkness on His headlong chase.

I could not gain; I could not lose. We stayed
Near, not closing nearer. I could hear the wind
Roaring through the turrets, fleshing out the flags;
Beggars' hands reached up from beggars' rags,
Doorways turned to rooms; we sped through rooms
To other doorways — eyes, hands, bare things numb
As gods in bas-relief. The rooms went on and on;
Neither of us stumbled as we ran.

My mind, like all minds, sought a single room without
Another doorway; or, another world beyond it.
In either place I could have turned and drawn
My dagger from my sash; I could have shown
The face beneath this hood. But as we passed
Each portal, sandals burning, thinking it the last,
One more, one more. His sandals raced before
And followed me across each stone slab floor.

**DICK ALLEN**

## *The Swing*

When I let go
  And way up there
Sat for a moment
  On thin air,

Feet dangling, hands
  Still shoulder-high,
I didn't hear
  Mother's cry

But only thought
  She'll love to see
Her offspring flying
  Crazily

Above her friends
  Across the yard;
I guess that's why she
  Pushed so hard.

## DICK ALLEN

# *Backstroking at Thrushwood Lake*

Momentary beds of white burst flowers
   Appear behind us. Kicking and pulling,
We continually create what disappears,
   So keep from drowning.
And what a sky is overhead! Great medieval blurs
   Of cumulus ascending.

We reenact da Vinci's naked man
   With four arms, four legs, fingertips
And feet in square and circle to explain
   Proportion. Or imagine hips
Rocking in a snowfield:  we have lain
   Down in snow, and left snow angel trails

From one side to the other, or a vertical
   String of paper dolls, joined head to toe across
Still waters. If we yell
   Out for the joy of it, or toss
Our heads from side to side, this spell
   Is exultation, just as it is madness.

Our elemental madness — that we know we live
   Today, this century, this year, this hour, minute
Everything is happening. Above,
   A flock of geese goes flying down towards Bridgeport.
Emerging in a high and cloudy cave,
   A Boeing's shadow is a crosslike print

To which you raise your head. The shore
　Is sand and willows — and our children
Floating near it, bobbing heads and figures
　Flattened on their plastic rafts. The wind
Blows them towards each other;
　Or away, unless they link their hands

While we tread water. Look at them. Their moments
　Also disappear, yet last — the paradox
Of memory. Think of mullein weeds,
　Full and empty pods upon their stalks,
Dead flowers and the living seeds,
　The washcloth texture of their flannel leaves,

And turn around. Stay close to me. Leave froth
　Again behind us and to both our sides.
Nothing ever will be beautiful enough
　Unless we're satisfied with how we ride
Waves backward and can love,
　For what we fashion, though we cannot keep, we need —

As I, these living moments, need the lake against
　My back, those towers in the clouds, the cries
Of children linking hands, the houses fenced
　About the lake, their windows brimmed with sky
Blue and white — trapped in the way your glance
　Catches me, and holds me, and all meanings fly.

# The "2" Train

*116<sup>th</sup> & Lennox*

Suppose you wake to a Bossa Nova song
somewhere in Spanish Harlem near the park;
suppose you sit in your bed and sing along,
watching the dawn fuss away the dark.
Suppose you rise, undress yourself, and shower,
staring into the mirror (unaware
how lovely you are), then spend another hour,
choosing your bright red dress and combing your hair.
Suppose you catch the train, like you always do,
to rumble underground for fifty blocks,
but suppose, today, the man across from you
is writing this poem on the top of a small white box.
Suppose he rises, holding a red red rose,
leans over, smiles, and says to you, "Suppose . . . ."

## *Andrew*

*Mark 1:17*

I well remember that we'd just begun
to cast our fishing nets into the sea,
and then I saw Him, in the mid-day sun,
standing there before us in Galilee.
Behold the One the Baptist bows before!
The One he calls the Lamb who'll set us free!
Then Jesus looked at us, from the shore,
we fishers of fish, and said, "Follow me."
Immediately, I dropped my heavy net,
and everything I had in Galilee,
and leapt out from the boat, without regret,
not even thinking what my future might be,
not even thinking, what could He possibly see
in a sweaty ignorant fisherman like me?

# *Eclipse*

*Matthew 27:45*

A crimson moon rises in the east
and blackens the burning sun, and soon
the soldiers will break my legs, and then the beast
of death will suffocate the afternoon.
But even here, half-dead, slumped in despair,
I hear His voice, and with my final breath,
cry out for mercy in a desperate prayer
to enter His kingdom, for life in the coming death.
Who then, with the voice of God, whispers: "This day,
you will be with me in paradise." I bow
my head, the earth begins to shudder and sway,
but salvation is right beside me, even now,
above the abyss, at the shores of the River Styx,
dying, like me, on a Roman crucifix.

WILLIAM BAER

# *The Shipmaster's Note*

*The Arctic*


*To whom it may concern*: we're trapped within
these everlasting ices of the north.
Tonight, I bother to dictate this note,
not because we might all starve and perish,
but because of what I've seen: madness.
The first one came two days ago, with sledge and dogs.
He keeps his distance but, at night,
I've heard him cry, "Come Victor, follow me."

The second one arrived today, half dead.
A doctor who'd tampered with the source of life,
conceived a creature in his own self-interest,
and then rejected the very one he'd made,
without compassion, without love. Despite
his health, he plans to chase his "daemon." Fine.
Let him go. This is the frozen place of death
for one such monster to pursue the other.

## *The Sawdust War*

On the early summer days I lay with back
against the sawdust pile and felt the heat
of a thousand pines, oaks, elms, sycamores
flowing into my flesh, my nose alive
with that peculiar smell of death the trees
became. Odd to me then how the summer rain
made the heat even more intense. Digging
down the dust, I began to reshape a world
I hardly knew:  the crumbly terrain became
theaters of the war. I was barely ten.

What I knew of the wide world and real war
came down the valley's road or flew over
the mountains I was caught between. Remote
I was nightly glued to the radio,
wondering at reports of a North African
campaign and Europe falling into chaos.
All daylight long I imitated what I
thought I heard, molding sawdust into hills,
roads, rivers, displacing troops of toys,
claiming ground by avalanche and mortar

fire, advancing bravely into black cities,
shrouding the fallen heroes with white bark.
I gained good ground against the Axis through
long summer days. Then one morning, dressed in
drab for hard work of war, I saw real smoke

rising from my battlefield. Crawling from
beneath the sawdust like vague spiderwebs,
claiming first the underground, then foxholes,
it spread like a wave of poison gas across
the woody hills I shaped with a mason's trowel.

I could not see the fire: it climbed from deep
within. No matter how I dug or shifted dust,
I could not find the source. My captured ground
nightly sank into itself. The gray smoke
hovered like owls under the slow stillness
of stars, until one night I woke to see,
at the center, a circle of smoldering sparks
turning to flame, ash spreading outward and down.
All night the pile glowed red, and I grew ashamed
for some fierce reason I could not then name.

## *Under the Tent*

The traveling show stretched its canvas
over the bluegrass behind the store
when we were ten, the last picture
shows we'd get to see during the war

the Axis forced on us. We crouched
by the flapping tent. The summer wind
at night was mischief in our heads,
blowing wild thyme in our hair. Then

we were full of war, those of us
too young to go. We claimed to know
all battlegrounds through hell and back.
What we wanted to do was throw

enough of the dark upon our skins
to slip beneath all tents unseen,
as the night patrol did in the film
we saw that summer before the end.

We had to time it right: to roll
exactly under the tent the way
you roll away from quick danger
in your sleep. Or we'd have to play

the fool when the tentwalker caught
us by the neck. Our detailed plan

precise, we penetrated the held
blackness the exact moment when

the light went out and the silver
screen lit up, rolling in unison
into farmers' heavy legs, spittle,
sleeping dogs, climbing into sound

and light, an illumination
we understood more than the real.
Such ecstasy of risk carried us
into ourselves and into the world.

# *From* Bombardier

### 1. Bathing in Lethe

He came back broader, taller, than I had
remembered, his duffel full of wonders
he gave to me:  compass, model B-17,
medals, ribbons, and silver wings. What's more
he made his aviator's cap fit my head.

For two green months that short summer we fished
the mountain creek across the open fields
our father plowed throughout the war. The bass
we caught he insisted we throw back, to
keep the stream alive he said. I wondered

why we walked the banks to try the deep pools
or shoals and why at dusk each day he stripped
and bathed so reverently in the spring-fed
stream while I thrashed about, torpedoing
a convoy of minnows or a frog. Now

I see I missed the mark. We bathed at home
with regularity. But the stream was
more than bath, more than an instrument
of cleanliness. The water sang a way
to be; the wind on ripples mapped our lives

with contours we couldn't see. Then my brother
was gone. The daily drone of planes from Tinker
Field told me he was gone again to war,
though in my mind I knew him bathing still
in a cool stream that washed most worry away.

3. MIA

The letters did not stop, and packages
periodically arrived for months after
the telegram. We knew the mail was slow,
but with fixed minds we saw him alive still
somewhere over there above the clouds bound
for places he would send us pieces of.

And then all stopped, and we began to think
of death camps that, before, we doubted ever
were, of how he might have glided in — to
crash into the walls to make a gate through which
the suffering could flee or simply to just be
there passing out mementos of the world.

No word ever came that he was found, nor
has it come. Forty-odd years and still I
feel him in the air, hear the sputter of
dying props that do not die, but whir on
into the dreams I have of this my life
that is also his life. Somewhere along

the lines of blood, it must be clearly written
we will not forget to honor the poetry

that daily then shaped those lives:  the lost children
of the holocaust singing through open flames,
the welcome home for those who stood it all,
the bombardier still on his one last run.

**JIM BARNES**

## *On Hearing the News That Hitler Was Dead*

When we heard the news that Hitler was dead,
under the porch something shook we couldn't find.
The dogs were by our sides, and all the hogs
were penned. The radio was full of Europe's end
and Berlin falling into Red Russia's hands.

The grown-ups heard it and sent us in the house
with the dogs, their bristles tough as quills.
Something big bumped against the floor and made
the blackest sounds we'd ever heard. Then, still
scraping underneath, it roared aloud until

we turned as white as chalk and someone fired
a shotgun into the dark beneath the floor.
We heard hell break from down below and burst
through the front-yard picket fence:  a panther
black as sin itself. They said it cleared a car

in one long leap and the ditch we couldn't jump.
We sighed and turned our normal brown as if
some threat of evil had missed us in the night.
The commentator's words on Hitler's death left
us puzzled about the course of war. A gift

of light was what we children waited for.
In the falling night we heard the far-off yowl

of wild cats in the woods, or thought we did.
The news leapt into the dark, wondering how
the master race so-called could master now

with Der Führer dead and the Russians drunk
on German schnapps. But what if he were not
the ashes they said were his? someone asked.
Silence and sound grew thick. Outside, lamplight
stumbled and fell into a starless night.

## RAY BRADBURY

# *To Ireland . . .*

I dare not go — that isle has ghosts
And spectral rains along the coasts
Such rains as weep their loss in tears
Till I am drowned in sunken years.
When last I walked a Dublin street,
My gaze was clear, my pulses fleet,
Now half a life or more is gone
I cannot face sad Dublin's dawn.
The book clerks who once waited me
Are grey and gaunt, how can that be?
The hotel staff has up and fled,
Some stay as haunts, the rest are dead.
The candy butchers, beggars, maids,
Sleep out beyond in Maynooth's shades,
O'Connell's harpists? Gone to stay
Deep strewn along the hills of Bray.
Their happy faces smoke and stream
Across my life to shape each dream
So, Ireland? No, I'll not return
Where ghosts in smoking rainfalls burn.
Through Dublin I'll not stroll again
I cannot stand that haunted rain
Where youngness melts away to sea
And kills my soul, my heart, and me.

# Go Not with Ruins in Your Mind

Go not with ruins in your mind
Or beauty fails; Rome's sun is blind
And catacomb your cold hotel
Where should-be heaven's could-be hell.
Beware the temblors and the flood
That time hides fast in tourist's blood
And shambles forth from hidden home
At sight of lost-in-ruins Rome.
Think of your joyless blood, take care,
Rome's scattered bricks and bones lie there
In every chromosome and gene
Lie all that was, or might have been.
All architectural tombs and thrones
Are tossed to ruin in your bones.
Time earthquakes there all life that grows
And all your future darkness knows,
Take not these inner ruins to Rome,
A sad man wisely stays at home;
For if your melancholy goes
Where all is lost, then your loss grows
And all the dark that self employs
Will teem — so travel then with joys.
Or else in ruins consummate
A death that waited long and late,
And all the burning towns of blood
Will shake and fall from sane and good,
And you with ruined sight will see

A lost and ruined Rome. And thee?
Cracked statue mended by noon's light
Yet innerscaped with soul's midnight.
So go not traveling with mood
Or lack of sunlight in your blood,
Such traveling has double cost,
When you and empire both are lost.
When your mind storm-drains catacomb,
And all seems graveyard rock in Rome —
Tourist, go not.
Stay home.
Stay home!

# *Byzantium I Come Not From*

Byzantium
I come not from
But from another time and place
Whose race is simple, tried and true;
As boy
I dropped me forth in Illinois,
A name with neither love nor grace
Was Waukegan. There I came from
And not, good friends, Byzantium.
And yet in looking back I see
From topmost part of farthest tree
A land as bright, beloved and blue
As any Yeats found to be true.
The house I lived in, hewn of gold
And on the highest market sold
Was dandelion-minted, made
By spendthrift bees in bee-loud glade.
And then of course our finest wine
Came forth from that same dandelion,
While dandelion was my hair
As bright as all the summer air;
I dipped in rainbarrels for my eyes
And cherries stained my lips, my cries,
My shouts of purest exaltation:
Byzantium? No. That Indian nation
Which made of Indian girls and boys
Spelled forth itself as Illinois.

Yet all the Indian bees did hum:
Byzantium.
Byzantium.

So we grew up with mythic dead
To spoon upon midwestern bread
And spread old gods' bright marmalade
To slake in peanut-butter shade.
Pretending there beneath our sky
That it was Aphrodite's thigh;
Pretending, too, that Zeus was ours
And Thor fell down in thundershowers.
While by the porch-rail calm and bold
His words pure wisdom, stare pure gold
My grandfather a myth indeed
Did all of Plato supersede;
While Grandmama in rocking-chair
Sewed up the raveled sleeve of care,
Crocheted cool snowflakes rare and bright
To winter us on summer night.
And uncles gathered with their smokes
Emitted wisdoms masked as jokes,
And aunts as wise as Delphic maids
Dispensed prophetic lemonades
To boys knelt there as acolytes
On Grecian porch on summer nights.
Then went to bed there to repent
The evils of the innocent
The gnat-sins sizzling in their ears
Said, through the nights and through the years
Not Illinois nor Waukegan

But blither sky and blither sun;
Though mediocre all our Fates
And Mayor not as bright as Yeats
Yet still we know ourselves. The sum?
Byzantium.
Byzantium.

## GWENDOLYN BROOKS

---

# *the preacher: ruminates behind the sermon*

*From* A Street in Bronzeville

I think it must be lonely to be God.
Nobody loves a master. No. Despite
The bright hosannas, bright dear-Lords, and bright
Determined reverence of Sunday eyes.

Picture Jehovah striding through the hall
Of His importance, creatures running out
From servant-corners to acclaim, to shout
Appreciation of His merit's glare.

But who walks with Him? — dares to take His arm,
To slap Him on the shoulder, tweak His ear,
Buy Him a Coca-Cola or a beer,
Pooh-pooh His politics, call Him a fool?

Perhaps — who knows? — He tires of looking down.
Those eyes are never lifted. Never straight.
Perhaps sometimes He tires of being great
In solitude. Without a hand to hold.

# *the children of the poor*

*From* The Womanhood

2.
What shall I give my children? who are poor,
Who are adjudged the leastwise of the land,
Who are my sweetest lepers, who demand
No velvet and no velvety velour;
But who have begged me for a brisk contour,
Crying that they are quasi, contraband
Because unfinished, graven by a hand
Less than angelic, admirable or sure.
My hand is stuffed with mode, design, device.
But I lack access to my proper stone.
And plenitude of plan shall not suffice
Nor grief nor love shall be enough alone
To ratify my little halves who bear
Across an autumn freezing everywhere.

# *We Real Cool*

*The Pool Players.*
*Seven at the Golden Shovel.*

We real cool. We
Left school. We

Lurk late. We
Strike straight. We

Sing sin. We
Thin gin. We

Jazz June. We
Die soon.

# GWENDOLYN BROOKS

## *From* Gay Chaps at the Bar

gay chaps at the bar

> *. . . and guys I knew in the States, young officers,*
> *return from the front crying and trembling. Gay*
> *chaps at the bar in Los Angeles, Chicago, New*
> *York . . .*
>
> *— Lieutenant William Couch*
> *in the South Pacific*

We knew how to order. Just the dash
Necessary. The length of gaiety in good taste.
Whether the raillery should be slightly iced
And given green, or served up hot and lush.
And we knew beautifully how to give to women
The summer spread, the tropics, of our love.
When to persist, or hold a hunger off.
Knew white speech. How to make a look an omen.
But nothing ever taught us to be islands.
And smart, athletic language for this hour
Was not in the curriculum. No stout
Lesson showed how to chat with death. We brought
No brass fortissimo, among our talents,
To holler down the lions in this air.

# GWENDOLYN BROOKS

piano after war

On a snug evening I shall watch her fingers,
Cleverly ringed, declining to clever pink,
Beg glory from the willing keys. Old hungers
Will break their coffins, rise to eat and thank.
And music, warily, like the golden rose
That sometimes after sunset warms the west,
Will warm that room, persuasively suffuse
That room and me, rejuvenate a past.
But suddenly, across my climbing fever
Of proud delight — a multiplying cry.
A cry of bitter dead men who will never
Attend a gentle maker of musical joy.
Then my thawed eye will go again to ice.
And stone will shove the softness from my face.


mentors

For I am rightful fellow of their band.
My best allegiances are to the dead.
I swear to keep the dead upon my mind,
Disdain for all time to be overglad.
Among spring flowers, under summer trees,
By chilling autumn waters, in the frosts
Of supercilious winter — all my days
I'll have as mentors those reproving ghosts.
And at that cry, at that remotest whisper,
I'll stop my casual business. Leave the banquet.
Or leave the ball — reluctant to unclasp her

Who may be fragrant as the flower she wears,
Make gallant bows and dim excuses, then quit
Light for the midnight that is mine and theirs.

# CATHARINE SAVAGE BROSMAN

## *Burning in Louvain*

*August 1914 — November 1917*

"Where one burns books, there in the end burn men" —
so Heine wrote. Thus Bruno's thought, before
the man himself was burnt, was set ablaze;
the learnéd works of Etienne Dolet,
thrice judged a heretic, twice caught, once charred,
were thrown into the fire; the holy wrath
of Torquemada and his ruffians
consigned both books and readers to the stake —

a cold, fanatical *auto-da-fé*. But more
than that: the wealth of learning in those tracts
went underground; obscurantism ruled;
and *it* was worse. Or so I thought, until
the Germans came. My God! The manuscripts,
the books that turned to ash — five hundred years
of learning, loveliness, devotion, labor, love!
From that, I'd made my life; they burnt my heart

along with parchments. Why? Before the war,
the Germans sent fine scholars here; the land
of Goethe, Schiller, Beethoven is theirs,
or *was*; their universities have been
a lamp for centuries. And what was gained
by shelling books? It was vindictive, not

# CATHARINE SAVAGE BROSMAN

just tactical: a boy, a patriot,
had shot an officer, and others fell

to bullets from the windows; at the rear
the column had been harassed. This was *war*,
however; what could they expect? They killed
three hostages — *bourgmestre*, citizens
of note — tossed bombs into the houses, burnt
magnificent creations of the past
in Gothic architecture, Flemish art,
and then attacked the library. I watched

the conflagration from my flat, the smoke,
the flames ascending as in images
of Armageddon, then the crumbling walls,
the crash, the floors collapsing into one
another, like a dream, the layers crushed,
unreal, together. In the exodus
toward the sea, the common things of life —
pathetic flotsam from the wreckage — bobbed

among the human waves that washed the roads —
old kettles, children's mattresses, a cage
without its bird. By chance I had at home,
entrusted to my care, a manuscript,
illuminated. As I left, I wrapped
it in a cloth, then threw it hastily
into my knapsack with a few old clothes,
some biscuits, cheese, and chocolate, a knife,

a bottle of Bordeaux. Along the route,
debris of incunabula and bits
of vellum drifted in the wind, still warm,
it seemed, their ragged edges curled and grey —
some letters visible withal, dark birds
ignited at the wing-tips, eyes on fire,
or angels weeping in a holocaust.
I had no plan, save exile somewhere — France

or England — still uncertain in the great
debacle. On the way toward Ghent, I found
by Providence a small iron chest, cast off
and empty, in a field. The woods nearby
were solitary: in the night I dug
a hole by scratching, dog-like, at the soil
and hacking roots. It was an offering
to past, and future, time. As if my work

had been fulfilled that night, I'll not survive,
I think, this awful war — too old, too ill.
Indeed, it may not end, but drag itself
from Ypres and Verdun to Passchendaele,
devouring everything, toward God knows what
unthinkable catastrophe, until
the last of Europe's blood and mind are gone,
as men decay, dissolve, or burn with books

they would not honor. My impulsive act,
the scribe's long labor — all seems useless now
amid the ruins. I cannot retrieve
the manuscript; the very woods may be

consumed and greater clouds of evil choke
the world, from thought turned diabolical,
as madmen light a pyre of words and flesh,
and set the stream of charity on fire.

# ROBERT DASELER

## *Night Fog*

You kissed me wetly on my mouth, and then
You pushed me out the door. Fog had spread
Up from the bay and thickly blanketed
The ghost-lit streets. This was the summer when,
Quarreling often, we blindly explored
"The shape of the elephant," which changed daily.
Along the Rose Walk the houselights glimmered palely
Beneath the night's damp gray laundry. Toward
The bottom of the slope I thought I heard
A muffled voice, perhaps a woman's, say
That something was heavy. The atmosphere
Was clammy, blurred, obscure. I couldn't hear
Distinctly, and I couldn't see my way,
But I walked on, prosperous and assured.

## *At the Barrier*

We said goodbye at the barrier,
And she slipped away. Carried along
On the stream, she soon was lost in the throng.
I waited to catch a last glimpse of her,
But in vain. She was gone. Sadder now
Than only an hour before, I turned
And walked back to my car. I have learned
A few things since that day: among them, how
To sleep alone and count myself as blessed
That I can still remember what it was
To be her lover. I was enchanted
In youth by destiny, that fearful quest
For gifts to hide my gaping faults and flaws,
For gifts — I little knew — already granted.

# ROBERT DASELER

## *14 Tamalpais Street*

I'd live, if I could, in the Berkeley hills
At 14 Tamalpais Street, a house
Of shingles, handsome still but tenebrous,
Where, in another time, two juveniles
Were sitting on the floor and playing board
Games — like Chinese checkers — whispering,
And kissing furtively. Everything
I know about those youngsters leads me toward
A kind of desperation of regret,
Emotion that grows sharper with the years.
When I look back on the chances won
And other chances lost, I can't forget
How many times my words provoked her tears
Or she took injury from what I'd done.

# ROBERT DASELER

## *Shadows*

I see you, darling, sitting on a bed
And pulling on a stocking, both legs bent
And one drawn up between the radiant
Window and me, your foot exhibited,
A silhouette inside an open space.
I'm on the shadow side of you, the light
Beyond is fuzzy, soft, and recondite,
Dying on your bosom, absent from your face.
I'm almost close enough to touch you, though
The gulf between us isn't one of distance.
Am I the man who took this picture of
Your stockinged legs some thirty years ago?
We range our lives about this dim persistence
Of things that are and have to be enough.

**JAMES DICKEY**

## *Reading* Genesis *to a Blind Child*

I am hiding beside you to tell you
What the world itself cannot show,
That you walk with an untold sight
Beyond the best reach of my light.
Try as you can to bear with me
As I struggle to see what you see
Be born of the language I speak.

Claw, feather, fur, and beak,
The beasts come under your hand
As into the Ark, from a land
That a cloud out of Hell must drown,
But for you, my second-born son.
The sheep, like your mother's coat,
The bear, the bird, and the goat

Come forth, and the cunning serpent.
I am holding my right arm bent
That you may take hold of the curve
Of round, warm skin that must serve
For evil. Now, unbreathing, I take
A pin, for the tooth of the snake.
You gravely touch it, and smile

Not at me, but into the world
Where you sit in the blaze of a book
With lion and eagle and snake

# JAMES DICKEY

Represented by pillow and pin,
By feathers from hats, and thin
Gull-wings of paper, loosed
From pages my fingers have traced

With the forms of free-flying birds;
And these are the best of my words.
If I were to ask you now
To touch the bright lid of my eye
Might I not see what you see?
Would my common brain not turn
To untellable vision, and burn

With the vast, creative color
Of dark, and the serpent, hidden forever
In the trembling right arm of your father,
Not speak? Can you take this book
And bring it to life with a look?
And can you tell me how
I have made your world, yet know

No more than I have known?
The beasts have smelled the rain,
Yet none has wailed for fear.
You touch me; I am here.
A hand has passed through my head,
And this is the hand of the Lord.
I have called forth the world in a word,

And am shut from the thing I have made.
I have loosed the grim wolf on the sheep;

# JAMES DICKEY

Yet upon the original deep
Of your innocence, they lie down
Together; upon each beast is a crown
Of patience, immortal and bright,
In which is God-pleasing delight.

Your grace to me is forbidden,
Yet I am remembering Eden
As you sit and play with a sword
Of fire, made of a word,
And I call through the world-saving gate
Each word creating your light:
All things in patient tones,

Birds, beasts, and flowering stones,
In each new word something new
The world cannot yet show.
All earthly things I have led
Unto your touch, have been fed
Thus on the darkness that bore them,
By which they most mightily shine,

And shall never know vision from sight,
Nor light from the Source of all light.
The sun is made to be hidden,
And the meaning and prospect of Eden
To go blind as a stone, until touched,
And the ship in a greenwood beached
Not rise through the trees on a smoke

# JAMES DICKEY

Of rain, till that flood break,
The sun go out in a cloud
And a voice remake it aloud,
Striving most gently to bring
A fit word to everything,
And to come on the thing it is seeking
Within its speaking, speaking.

**JAMES DICKEY**

# *On the Hill Below the Lighthouse*

Now I can be sure of my sleep;
I have lost the blue sea in my eyelids.
From a place in the mind too deep
For thought, a light like a wind is beginning.
  *Now I can be sure of my sleep.*

When the moon is held strongly within it,
The eye of the mind opens gladly.
Day changes to dark, and is bright,
And miracles trust to the body,
  *When the moon is held strongly within it.*

A woman comes true when I think her.
Her eyes on the window are closing.
She has dressed the stark wood of a chair.
Her form and my body are facing.
  *A woman comes true when I think her.*

Shade swings, and she lies against me.
The lighthouse has opened its brain.
A browed light travels the sea.
Her clothes on the chair spread their wings.
  *Shade swings, and she lies against me.*

Let us lie in returning light,
As a bright arm sweeps through the moon.
The sun is dead, thinking of night

Swung round like a thing on a chain.
*Let us lie in returning light.*

Let us lie where your angel is walking
In shadow, from wall onto wall,
Cast forth from your off-cast clothing
To pace the dim room where we fell.
*Let us lie where your angel is walking,*

Coming back, coming back, going over.
An arm turns the light world around
The dark. Again we are waiting to hover
In a blaze in the mind like a wind
*Coming back, coming back, going over.*

*Now I can be sure of my sleep;*
*The moon is held strongly within it.*
*A woman comes true when I think her.*
*Shade swings, and she lies against me.*
*Let us lie in returning light;*
*Let us lie where your angel is walking,*
*Coming back, coming back, going over.*

# *The Island*

A light come from my head
Showed how to give birth to the dead
That they might nourish me.
In a wink of the blinding sea
I woke through the eyes, and beheld
No change, but what had been,
And what cannot be seen
Any place but a burnt-out war:
The engines, the wheels, and the gear
That bring good men to their backs
Nailed down into wooden blocks,
With the sun on their faces through sand,
And polyps a-building the land
Around them of senseless stone.
The coral and I understood
That these could come to no good
Without the care I could give,
And that I, by them, must live.
I clasped every thought in my head
That bloomed from the magical dead,
And seizing a shovel and rake,
Went out by the ocean to take
My own sweet time, and start
To set a dead army apart.
I hammered the coffins together
Of patience and hobnails and lumber,
And gave them names, and hacked

Deep holes where they were stacked.
Each wooden body, I took
In my arms, and singingly shook
With its being, which stood for my own
More and more, as I laid it down.
At the grave's crude, dazzling verge
My true self strained to emerge
From all they could not save
And did not know they could give.
I buried them where they lay
In the brass-bound heat of the day,
A whole army lying down
In animal-lifted sand.
And then with rake and spade
I curried each place I had stood
On their chests and on their faces,
And planted the rows of crosses
Inside the blue wind of the shore.
I hauled more wood to that ground
And a white fence put around
The soldiers lying in waves
In my life-giving graves.
And a painless joy came to me
When the troopships took to the sea,
And left the changed stone free
Of all but my image and me:
Of the tonsured and perilous green
With its great, delighted design
Of utter finality,
Whose glowing workman stood
In the intricate, knee-high wood

## JAMES DICKEY

In the midst of the sea's blind leagues,
Kicked off his old fatigues,
Saluted the graves by their rank,
Paraded, lamented, and sank
Into the intelligent light,
And danced, unimagined and free,
Like the sun taking place on the sea.

## RHINA P. ESPAILLAT

# On Being Accused of Optimism After Predicting Good Weather

I meant to tell you how the light may turn
like notes plucked on a string tuned up a hair;
how calibrations country people learn
to make, measure the thinning of the air;
how suddenly a field bullied by rain
roils with dissent and rises to be heard;
how turncoat leaf by leaf the birch makes plain
from what elusive shade the sun's inferred.
I meant to tell you, but the moment passed.
It was your face whose landscape — restless eyes
darkened by scudding thoughts and overcast
with unspent weather — took me by surprise
so wholly that I turned and looked away,
forgetting what I meant, or meant to say.

# *Breath*

> *God's breath in man returning to his birth,*
> *The soul in paraphrase . . .*
> > *"Prayer," George Herbert*

How hard and with what patience have I tried
to sing like you, George Herbert, make of prayer
a song of praise in which to bless, confide,
surrender without blame, like you, who bare
yourself to God and lie down in His hand
as on a bed that Love prepares for you.
You never question, rage to understand
the secrets He withholds from us. I do,
and spoil my every word, however meek
I struggle to become, with asking why,
with calling to account, before I die,
the Breath that lets you sing but bids me speak.
Who is to blame, if what I speak is wrong?
Unless that Breath turns all my speech to song.

## *At the Buffet*

> *Because I could not stop for Death —*
> *He kindly stopped for me —*
> > *— Emily Dickinson*

As if life were a house you were shown through
so quickly you could not sit down at all,
you drift, at first, from room to room, the view
from this terrace and that shifting, each wall
another landscape: someone's taste not quite
your own, but interesting by day, you think,
odd angles, these refractions of the light
in shades you would not choose, gray, salmon pink.

You wonder how the footprint of this place —
an odd phrase for a dwelling! — looks, or would
look, if you regarded it from space
as birds do.                    Then you spot him, in a good
but unpretentious suit with worn lapels,
a thin white blade of cuff, raw knuckles, rough
nails not wholly clean. Over the smells
of wine and cheese, an odor rank enough —
garden or farm? — to make you turn. Small talk
about Charles Ives, the parking in New York.

Bald, a bit seedy, but you know him: he's
"the man in the black sweats," says a good line

in some remembered poem. And he sees
the recognition in your eyes, the sign.
Silly, that other image, flowing cape,
dark hood and scythe. This is the sober dress
in which he works the crowd:  no force, no rape,
not even mild seduction. And some less
diffident figure draws your eyes away
to new configurations, coffee, cake.

An hour later, with the light of day
leached out of every window, time to shake
the crumbs out of your lap; you're tired; you need
to climb out of these shoes; you need your bed.
And there he leans — as if you had agreed
on hour and place — against the door, his head
cocked patiently, not lover, no, not friend,
but there, to take you home at party's end.

## *Turning Forty*

The barroom mirror lit up with our wives
has faded to a loaded-to-the-gills
Japanese subcompact, little lives
asleep behind us, heading for the hills

in utter darkness through invisible
countryside we know by heart by light;
but woods that are humane and hospitable
often turn eerie on a moonless night.

Our talk is quiet: the week's triumphs, failings,
gossip, memories — but largely fears.
In our brief repertoire of poses ailing's
primary, and more so with the years

now every step seems haunted by the future,
not only ours, but all that they will face:
a stricter world, with scarceness for a teacher,
bad air, bad water, no untrammeled space —

or so it seems to us, after the Fall,
but for the young the world is always new.
Maybe that's what dates us worst of all
and saves them: What we'll miss they never knew.

We're old enough now to be old enough,
to know what loss is — not just hair and breath;

each has eyeballed reality by now:
a rift, a failure, or a major death.

They landed on us; we were not consulted,
although our darkest yearnings aren't so deep.
Let's tick off the short wish list of adulthood:
sleep, honor, sleep, love, riches, sleep, and sleep . . .

and camaraderie, that warms the blood,
the mildest, most forgiving form of love.
In an uncertain world a certain good
is one who'll laugh off what you're leery of.

That's why we're out here, racing with the clock
through cold and darkness:  so that, glass in hand,
we'll face our half-life, padded for the shock
by a few old souls who understand.

Now the odometer, uncompromising,
shows all its nines' tails hanging in the air.
Now an entire row of moons is rising,
rising, rising, risen — we are there:

Total Maturity. The trick is how
to amortize remorse, desire, and dread.
Eyes ahead, companions:  Life is Now.
The serious years are opening ahead.

# JONATHAN GALASSI

## *Siren*

In your think tank you're Olympia,
all languid length and skin and two red roses
budding in the suds; or you're unhappy, a
sea fury frozen in your fountain poses.
And then a fine rime settles on the water,
hides you almost, Susannah, soaped to gleaming,
but wise from birth to what the elders taught her,
that though the tongue be stone the spirit's scheming
heat and action, craves to be
swimming with you into infinity —
as on those evenings when I hear you run
your bath and put your hair up in a bun
and sigh, and sink into your second home,
and then you call me from the other room.

# JONATHAN GALASSI

## *Hymn*

Will I meet you in the heaven
that I don't believe in, where
each of us is given
and forgiven our life here,

granted the fulfillment
of original desire,
forgiven the consumption
of ourselves in the world's fire?

In my dream I'm waking
in an unmown field, alone,
and everything is glistening
because the rain has gone.

I can hear the high weeds bending.
They are letting someone pass.
Is it you? I see us heading
to the same place on the grass.

Will we travel through each other
or reconstitute as one?
Will each truly see the other,
be the other in this sun?

I know what I have dreamed of
that my hasty heart has wrecked:

the paradise where parallel
intentions intersect,

the otherwhere I live for —
can it be the same for you?
It's against the laws of physics
and metaphysics, too.

But in the dream I'm dreaming
neither interferes.
Your defenseless eyes are searching,
I am open, and in tears.

There's no motion, no commotion,
only birdsong breaking through.
In the world I don't believe in
nothing's keeping me from you.

## R. S. GWYNN

# *Cléante to Elmire*

Rising, Madame, towards heaven in a bed
That elevates my knees and lifts my head
To sustenance, that is, a plastic tray
Of Jell-O, applesauce, and consommé,
I have become a connoisseur of juice,
Which leaves me liquid, not to mention *loose*,
And keeps my precious fluids running clear
Until such time as I shall disappear —
Like what descends transparently for pain,
Dripping, *ex machina*, to tubes that drain.
What has, you may well ask, contributed
To this apostrophe to one long dead
From one so nearly so? You come to me,
As Sting might say, in *synchronicity*;
Searching just now for bulletins about
This storm called *Cara* which, I have no doubt,
Shall live up to its namesake, namely *you*,
And do us in before the day is through,
I channel-surfed and lit on PBS.
My dear, shall I be coy and make you guess
What stopped me there and brought a hurricane
And you into one focus in my brain?
One line, in Mr. Wilbur's fine translation:
*And cultivate a sober moderation. . . .*
Think of it! If we ever needed proof
Of greater patterns, wasn't it *Tartuffe*
That brought us once and brings us now together —

Molière and two lost souls and raging weather?
Lord, twenty years have passed and still each line
Smacks tartly on the tongue like a good wine
Heady with epigram and foiled seduction.

It was The Coastal Players' great production —
Rhymed verse they said our audience could not
Make much of, let alone digest the plot —
Yet how we triumphed, I the *raisonneur*
Cléante and you the faithful spouse, the pure
Elmire, the model of a perfect wife.
So much for art. Who says it mirrors life?
Like leaves whirling outside, the years have flown
And taken with them Pernelle and Orgon.
Dorine the maid (Remember? What a bitch!)
Went into real estate and came out rich,
Sweet Marianne had children and grew fat,
And you'd have thought it less than fitting that
The charge against Tartuffe, so like the play's,
Was finally dropped: not only virtue pays.
In spite of the applause I found so sweet
I never found the courage to repeat
Those evenings' glories in another play.
And you? We gathered you were on your way
To greater things. A touring company
(*A Chorus Line!*) had called, you gushed to me
At the cast party, and our toasts went on
(Fuck "sober moderation"!) until dawn,
When I appeared, bedraggled, in your gown —
My coming out, no small thing in this town —
Battering Blanche against your not-so-manly

# R. S. GWYNN

Peruked and powdered parody of Stanley
While Matt, your surly boyfriend, hulked and glared.
You laughed at him. I must say *I* was scared.

After that night our paths diverged. I learned
Your offers never came, heard that you'd turned
To wilder exploits, but, then, I was so
Into my own pursuits I didn't know
How dark your path became. Often our cars
Would pass en route to our respective bars.
We'd honk and wave like drunken teens. Dare I
Hope that one kiss I blew you said good-bye?
Your end came the next summer. Tom, the cop
Who'd played Laurent, came by the flower shop
To tell me what he knew — in rapid order,
Marriage, your panicked calls — quick as the border
Of this new storm front alters. Drugs, of course,
Were much of it, and there was the divorce
Which had turned ugly. Still, the Lord knows what
Led to that final beating and the shot
That tore your face away — before Matt made
The 911 call, sobbing while he played
His own death scene. I only pray it's true
What Tom believed himself: he said that you
Were dead already when the shot was fired.

My own death is the kind that is "acquired,"
Which makes it sound like something one might paste
Into a book, as one "acquires" a taste
For sherry, leather scenes, or the ballet.
All prance around the piper. All must pay.

No more of that. The plot by now is stale.
Let Tony Kushner live to tell the tale
And garner all the money and awards.
May *my* audition be one aiming towards
A long run somewhere in a stellar cast
In which no bow I take will be my last.
Corny? You know me, Cara, for I am
The same as you, eternally a ham
Who holds out hopes of One who can explain,
A *Raisonneur* of happiness and pain,
Who proves for us that love is possible
And need not climax in so great a fall
As what we've suffered . . . and that The Machine
Will lower with a Prince who makes us clean
And whole again, who lends His blessed grace
To salve my wreckage and restore your face —
Who lets the memory of a dead friend's laugh,
In the dark valley, be my rod and staff.
In a world full of such unwelcome guests
As storms, Tartuffe, and sickness, small requests.

It makes a curious *dénouement* that I,
Too ill for anything except to die,
May be evacuated, which shall save
These sodden relics for a drier grave.
The winds are rising, Cara, your own winds
With the great closing curtain that descends
Upon us as we play our games again
With tracking charts and crayons. CNN
Leads the hour with your great whirling eye.
Live oaks and sweetgums just outside my high

# R. S. GWYNN

Window gesticulate the *agon* for us
As fiercely as a Sophoclean chorus.
The living board their windows, and their eyes
Lift past their fragile rooflines to the skies.
*What wind is this?* they ask themselves.

                                    I say
It is the wind that bears the world away.

# R. S. GWYNN

## *Laird of the Maze*

Despite he was a frog and relished flies,
His personality possessed no taint.
No warmth flowed in his veins; he suffered this,
But none that knew him could have thought him evil.
Was lackey to no vices; but one joy, his penchant
For moonlit swimming at the maze's center.
At midnight sought his native element,
The pool of scum. None saw his nakedness.

That maze was Life! All others wandered there
Seeking to solve its puzzle; only he
Construed the pattern of its form in abstract
And bore it like the impress of a signet,
For the hedges of that maze were darkly lush
And knit so thickly as to seem impenetrable.
There one could hear the Master at his pleasure —
The dull splash of a dishrag being slapped.

The pathways of his argument, his wit,
The winding traverse of his metaphors,
His irony and syntax, like the maze,
Confounded all, myself among the least.
Yet I must try to . . . true, he were a frog,
But a kindred soul lay cloaked beneath that green skin:
Idealist, poet, scholar, who lacked only
The spark of camaraderie, the firm handshake.

## R. S. GWYNN

So years I lay here in this crumbling tower
Waiting for moonrise and the loathsome croak
Of the frog-man's nightly cry for company.
Mere silence echoes now. The pool is still,
As I gaze into my shoe, which contains a foot,
As I try to piece together what his life meant:
Fallen, the rightful laird, last of his line,
A slick spot drying on the courtyard stone.

# R. S. GWYNN

## *The Drive-In*

Under the neon sign he stands,
My father, tickets in his hands.
Now it is my turn; all the while,
Knee-deep in stubs he tries to smile,
Crying, *You'll love it. Slapstick. Fights.*
*One dollar, please. Please dim your lights.*
I pay and enter. Mother waits
In a black truck with dangling plates
And snag-toothed grillwork idling there
On the front row. She combs her hair
And calls for me to take my place.
The moon-lights dying on her face,
She lights another cigarette
And starts to sing the alphabet.
Quickly, I turn the speaker on:
The soundtrack is a steady drone
Of snoring. With his pockets full
My father gathers up his wool,
His pink tongue rolling up and down.
A wolf, dainty in hat and gown,
Appears, sneaking across the screen
Above my father. Then the scene
Expands to show a flock of sheep.
The wolf is drooling. In his sleep
My father smiles, my mother sighs,
And dabbing gently at her eyes
She goes across to sniff his breath.

# R. S. GWYNN

A shepherd clubs the wolf to death,
The sheep dance lightly in the sun,
And now the feature has begun:
*Union Pacific* is its name.
I know it, know it frame by frame,
The tyranny of separation,
The lack of all communication
From shore to shore, the struggle through
Smashed chairs and bottles toward the true
Connection of a spike of gold.
I fall asleep. The night is cold.
And waking to the seat's chill touch
I hear the last car's slipping clutch,
And on the glass a veil of frost
Obscures this childhood I have lost.
The show is over. Time descends.
And no one tells me how it ends.

# *Last Trip to Greece*

I had the labels ready with their essence:
Add water, serve. Light, language, beauty, sea,
body, etcetera, etcetera. Time.
In honesty I need to change the tune:
queasiness, boredom, and misogyny.
Forget the little table by the sea
under an awning. Stupefied by sun,
we were to have sat musing over dreams
dreamed in the shuttered twilight of siestas.
No. There was sitting, though — sitting and waiting.
Minutes ticked by. The sluggish month of June
little by little shifted its big bulk,
morning to evening, dawn to afternoon,
till it was time to climb back on the plane.

The very language was to have been a spell
I'd left half woven, alien, magical,
testing the murky waters with my tongue . . .
Ha! I remembered everything too well.
Words meant the culture that they dragged along.
I entered it each time I acquiesced
to vowels and consonants and all the rest.
The language had three genders, it was true,
but only one that mattered. What was new
was how I saw this world as one of men.
The energy was men's, men's was the joy:
the sun-dark muscles at the soccer match

# RACHEL HADAS

matched the colossal kouros' marble thigh,
the only thing of beauty in Vathy —

skillfully rendered, lovingly observed,
alert and timeless in its stony way.
But these were partial pleasures — half a world.
Where was the realm of women? Where was I?
Could all we weaker vessels be boiled down
to that one expedition to the convent?
We rose so early sun and moon still shared the sky
to climb the mountain, find the nuns halfway
to heaven, but beyond the reach of time,
of energy clocked by sinew or by speed.
With their cracked bells, devotions, goats, and hens,
their sanctuary of bees and running water,
their milk and ouzo offered thirsty travelers,
do they have all of paradise they need?

I wasn't made to live in paradise.
And I'd this misconception about time.
The precious element became a baggy
garment in whose folds I nearly smothered,
however fervently I'd dreamed of it
before I put it on. For too much time
is like a swirling cloak without an opening.
You cannot use your arms to work, you almost
go down like Agamemnon in the bath
speared by his furious consort Clytemnestra,
that queen whose weapon bridged two worlds with blood —
and whom, although I thought I knew the myth,
I grew to be more sympathetic with.
Oh, everything had changed! Or was it simply me?

# RACHEL HADAS

Idées reçues I'd readily affixed
to nature like a pair of rosy lenses
had somehow come undone. The gentle sheep bells
tinkling on Acrocorinth when I first
visited the place ten years ago
still tintinnabulated; but this time
what made the day was an enormous snake
sliding into a hole. He owned the place.
He — but why he? What sex are guardian serpents?
And who was I? Well, newly pregnant; queasy;
uneasy in the combat zone I kept
perceiving between what were now two worlds,
the fight a sudden struggle in my gut.
Oh god, how much I wanted to go home!

Urgency was the measure of regret
for what I'd had and seen and lost and learned;
of hope, as well, for what I was becoming,
for what I needed distance to make true.
Dreams meanwhile took on firm geometries:
one family member wedged into each corner,
the loaded silence palpable between them
as I took courage, made my brief announcement,
and shattered certain symmetries for good.
Forever. Change on both sides, in the middle;
change in my middle. I wasn't pedestaled,
entranced in a museum; nor did I float
dreamily above the pool of time.
All the old lineaments were ripe for change.

# RACHEL HADAS

## *Along Edges*

*to Mark Rudman*

*The poet is the true and only doctor.*
*— Emerson*

Scientist of mourning, doctor, teach
me your categories. Which is which —
the tragic and the comic and bizarre
melting to one, the fishing boat, the bar,
the fearful father shining like a star?
You see beyond the visual, you know.
Each meaning yields its antitype to you:
life out of death and nothing out of all.
Blackness that opened with your father's fall
spreads into a dark screen against which glow
those paltry episodes we glibly call
the present. In your presence, hovering things
materialize — but not to fold their wings,
perch on a shoulder. No, they prophesy
scenes off limits to the daily eye.
Funny or uncanny, wild or tame,
your rapt abstraction holds you just the same.
Give you a death and even as you grieve,
you pull life like a bright scarf from your sleeve,
wave it once vaguely in the cloudy air —
soon memories are showing everywhere.
The ordinary opens its dull door,

no violence is alien any more,
your golden son is dancing on a tomb
you traveled far to see but fear to climb.
You see yourself at twenty; equally
see all our absences a century
from now, when not a single soul of all
our cohorts will be here. For good or ill,
now is our time, this strange earth is our place.
Each present moment like a glint of ice
above opacities of ocean shows
deeper intimations from below.
With so much dimly grasped at, how can all
be somehow seen and understood? You feel
the double pull of gravity and joy
and felt it years ago, a lawless boy
out in pursuit of knowledge, drink, or sin,
wandering along edges looking in.

Poet of mounds and ruins, prairies, caves,
of deserts glittering in the sun's raw waves,
of childhood asthma and of city snow,
Riverside Park and Courbet's studio,
the unmade movie always being shot
at the sheer cliff's side, whether "real" or not,
I send you greetings from my patch of green,
magician of the seen and the unseen,
to whom the truth of memory adheres
through country stillnesses and city fears.
Seeing your lit window, I can tell
the war against oblivion's going well.
The spotlight of your desk lamp is a clue
to secrets I will learn of first from you.

# RACHEL HADAS

## *Super Nivem*

*Asperges me hyssopo, et super nivem dealbabor.*
*Psalm LI*

My scars are slow in healing, dark
thin crowns of wound where none should be,
marring what wraps me, marring me.

I am not sad at anything,
not stung, but scars remember more
and make me veteran of a war

I fought forgetting. Stenciled on
wide unresisting planes of skin,
they trace my alphabet of sin,

the language undeciphered still.
But clotted letters I can read.
They mark the parts of me that bleed.

## *Benefit Night, New York City Ballet*

Once in its mannered mode
the dance appeared to me
a dusty stiff brocade
of faded mystery.

But this was years ago.
Later it came to seem
a vain if gallant blow
aimed at the cruel regime

of time and gravity
by beauty to defy
the merciless decree:
we grow old, sicken, die.

The years that press us down
carve sullen masks of age.
Eyes fixed on the dim ground,
we creep across our stage.

Now sitting here with you
in the enchanted dark
I still hold to this view.
The sweating dancers work

lightly to lift a great
somber collective pall —

mortality's dead weight —
from you and me and all

who, separate, doomed, and dumb,
can drink in nonetheless
our share of the sublime.
The dancers dance for us:

our grief, love, vanity.
Their bodies form a screen
between humanity
and the pull of the unseen.

The burdens we all bear,
great or small, find ease
this evening in the sheer
radiance of disguise.

For as we raptly gaze
at limbs in cool blue light
sculpting a carnal maze
of intricate delight,

of passions sketched on air,
it is ourselves we see,
divested of despair.
You turn and smile at me.

# ANTHONY HECHT

## *The End of the Weekend*

A dying firelight slides along the quirt
Of the cast-iron cowboy where he leans
Against my father's books. The lariat
Whirls into darkness. My girl, in skin-tight jeans,
Fingers a page of Captain Marryat,
Inviting insolent shadows to her shirt.

We rise together to the second floor.
Outside, across the lake, an endless wind
Whips at the headstones of the dead and wails
In the trees for all who have and have not sinned.
She rubs against me and I feel her nails.
Although we are alone, I lock the door.

The eventual shapes of all our formless prayers,
This dark, this cabin of loose imaginings,
Wind, lake, lip, everything awaits
The slow unloosening of her underthings.
And then the noise. Something is dropped. It grates
Against the attic beams.
                                        I climb the stairs,

Armed with a belt.
                                A long magnesium strip
Of moonlight from the dormer cuts a path
Among the shattered skeletons of mice.
A great black presence beats its wings in wrath.

# ANTHONY HECHT

Above the boneyard burn its golden eyes.
Some small grey fur is pulsing in its grip.

# ANTHONY HECHT

## *The Ghost in the Martini*

Over the rim of the glass
Containing a good martini with a twist
I eye her bosom and consider a pass,
    Certain we'd not be missed

In the general hubbub.
Her lips, which I forgot to say, are superb,
Never stop babbling once (Aye, there's the rub)
    But who would want to curb

Such delicious, artful flattery?
It seems she adores my work, the distinguished grey
Of my hair. I muse on the salt and battery
    Of the sexual clinch, and say

Something terse and gruff
About the marked disparity in our ages.
She looks like twenty-three, though eager enough.
    As for the famous wages

Of sin, she can't have attained
Even to union scale, though you never can tell.
Her waist is slender and suggestively chained,
    And things are going well.

The martini does its job,
God bless it, seeping down to the dark old id.

# ANTHONY HECHT

("Is there no cradle, Sir, you would not rob?"
  Says ego, but the lid

Is off. The word is Strike
While the iron's hot.) And now, ingenuous and gay,
She is asking me about what I was like
  At twenty. (Twenty, eh?)

You wouldn't have liked me then,
I answer, looking carefully into her eyes.
I was shy, withdrawn, awkward, one of those men
  That girls seemed to despise,

Moody and self-obsessed,
Unhappy, defiant, with guilty dreams galore,
Full of ill-natured pride, an unconfessed
  Snob and a thorough bore.

Her smile is meant to convey
How changed or modest I am, I can't tell which,
When I suddenly hear someone close to me say,
  "You lousy son-of-a-bitch!"

A young man's voice, by the sound,
Coming, it seems, from the twist in the martini.
"You arrogant, elderly letch, you broken-down
  Brother of Apeneck Sweeney!

Thought I was buried for good
Under six thick feet of mindless self-regard?
Dance on my grave, would you, you galliard stud,
  Silenus in leotard?

# ANTHONY HECHT

Well, summon me you did,
And I come unwillingly, like Samuel's ghost.
*'All things shall be revealed that have been hid.'*
*There's* something for you to toast!

You only got where you are
By standing upon my ectoplasmic shoulders,
And wherever that is may not be so high or far
In the eyes of some beholders.

Take, for example, me.
I have sat alone in the dark, accomplishing little,
And worth no more to myself, in pride and fee,
Than a cup of luke-warm spittle.

But honest about it, withal . . ."
("Withal," forsooth!) "Please not to interrupt.
And the lovelies went by, 'the long and the short and the tall,'
Hankered for, but untupped.

Bloody monastic it was.
A neurotic mixture of self-denial and fear;
The verse halting, the cataleptic pause,
No sensible pain, no tear,

But an interior drip
As from an ulcer, where, in the humid deep
Center of myself, I would scratch and grip
The wet walls of the keep,

Or lie on my back and smell
From the corners the sharp, ammoniac, urine stink.
*'No light, but rather darkness visible.'*
And plenty of time to think.

In that thick, fetid air
I talked to myself in giddy recitative:
*'I have been studying how I may compare
This prison where I live*

*Unto the world . . .'* I learned
Little, and was awarded no degrees.
Yet all that sunken hideousness earned
Your negligence and ease.

Nor was it wholly sick,
Having procured you a certain modest fame;
A devotion, rather, a grim device to stick
To something I could not name."

Meanwhile, she babbles on
About men, or whatever, and the juniper juice
Shuts up at last, having sung, I trust, like a swan.
Still given to self-abuse!

Better get out of here;
If he opens his trap again it could get much worse.
I touch her elbow, and, leaning toward her ear,
Tell her to find her purse.

# *Death Sauntering About*

The crowds have gathered here by the paddock gates
And racing silks like the flags of foreign states
   Billow and snap in the sun,
And thoroughbreds prance and paw the turf, the race
Is hotly contested, for win and show and place,
   Before it has yet begun.

The ladies' gowns in corals and mauves and reds,
Like fluently-changing variegated beds
   Of a wild informal garden,
Float hither and yon where gentlemen advance
Questions of form, the inscrutable ways of chance,
   As edges of shadow harden.

Among these holiday throngs, a passer-by,
Mute, unremarked, insouciant, saunter I,
   One who has placed —
Despite the tumult, the pounding of hooves, the sweat,
And the urgent importance of everybody's bet —
   No premium on haste.

# A. M. JUSTER

# Harapha's Counsel to the Philistines

*He will directly to the lords, I fear,*
*And with malicious counsel stir them up*
*Some way or other yet further to afflict thee.*
*"Samson Agonistes"*

Distinguished lords, our triumph is complete;
The force of wit has overcome brute force.
The rebel Samson will not terrorize
Our lands, seduce our women, or insult
Our gods again. Shackles are a mere
Precaution, since his sight and will are spent.
He is reduced to braying raspy threats;
It is as if that vaunted jaw could speak.
The spells of sorcerers no longer charm
His form; he wallows in the filth
Much like a pig he would not deign to eat.
While we must not forget our valiant dead,
I know that they would want us to enjoy
This blessed day.
                    Accordingly, I call
For celebration — music, feasting, dance
And Samson on display for all to see.
Let laborers and slaves be free from toil,
Let casks of wine be opened in the streets
And let the butchers ready bulls and goats.
Prepare the temple for a great event
And send our strongest soldiers to retrieve

Our trophy.
                But as we rejoice, my lords,
Remember that the fairest prize is not
Our captive, but the peace his capture brings.
 The conscripts can return to work the fields;
We can once more attempt to build a realm
More mighty than the world has ever seen.
They will not frighten children in their beds
Or women chastely guarding home and hearth.
Their magistrates will once again profess
Allegiance to our land, and they will pay
Us for the damage done by acts of war.
Rejoice, my lords, the gods stand by our side.
Tell the high priest to make an offering
Greater than any he has made before.
We have subdued the brutish infidel,
And we shall hear no more from Israel.

## *Fugitive Son*

The Japanese mourn children they abort.
In Shinto shrines they pick a figurine
To represent the life that they cut short.
They bow, then slide a folded note between
The sandalwood and jade as if a soul
That never loved a face could now forgive
Or any act of penance could control
Unwanted visits from a fugitive.

I never picked a message I could send
Or bargained for forgiveness. There was none.
Although I know my boy does not intend
More pain, he asks about the nameless son
We lost three months before he was conceived.
I have no words to tell him how we grieved.

## *How We Got to Elmira*

She must have been attracted to faithless men;
he voted for Democrats to feel betrayed.
We packed efficiently and on short notice.
While searching for exits, he would always grin
and tell us that the next house would have a deck,
another bathroom or view of a lake.

He wanted places that clamored for his goods,
that kept his taxes low, and that zoned out jerks.
Although I always told him I understood,
I kept returning to that first town we left,
which grew more idyllic every time we moved.
I nearly recalled a life I never lived.

She believed him when he said our break would come,
the crisis of the moment was sure to pass.
I remember her confiding she had dreamed
about a speech he'd make; in it he expressed
his debt to her for his enormous success
and for remaining with him in the hard times.

He was off on a supposed business trip
when she packed up everything and took us north
to live with family. We could not discuss
him very much; his name was our nakedness,
sometimes essential but still a source of shame.
When we heard he died we had to check the map.

# A. M. JUSTER

## *On Remembering Your Funeral Was Today*

When I first swore to tap-dance on your grave,
My oath was neither wit nor metaphor.
Still hell-bent on far more, my war goes on
Although your other enemies forgave.

Don't think your death prevents an evened score,
Or I will weary of this marathon,
For while my daily rage may be diminished,
I assure you we are still not finished.

I bet by now that you have stolen time
To edit *The Beginner's Guide To Hell.*

I trust you've cheated Charon of a dime
And somehow brought a blush to Jezebel.

I see you basting in satanic slime
Before deep-frying in your cockroach shell.

# A. M. JUSTER

## *Letter to Auden*

Uh, Wystan?
            Please forgive my arrogance;
You know how most Americans impose.
Your chat with Byron gave me confidence
    That your Platonic ghost would not oppose
    Some verse disturbing you from your repose.
Besides, there's time to kill now that the Lord
Has silenced Merrill and his ouija board.

Or do you pine for peace in Paradise,
    Besieged by every half-baked psychic hack
Intent on mining gems from your advice?
    With me, please don't insist on writing back
    Unless you can't resist some biting crack.
I also recognize that I had better
Keep my remarks far shorter than your *Letter*.

Indeed, I'll need substantial guile and nerve
    To try to emulate your bracing pace.
At twenty-nine, your lines had style and verve;
    My work at thirty-nine seems commonplace
    And foreordained to sink without a trace.
In any case, I do not hold out hope
Of sharing space with you or spiteful Pope.

A partial consolation on bad days
    Is no contemporary can compete

With you at all. Downtrodden MFA's
　　Denounce the Audenesque as obsolete
Oppression by your dead-white-male elite,
　　But then they go on to become depressed
　　Because there's nothing left to be confessed.

Only a few eccentrics still support
　　Those poets who can scan lines properly.
However, I'm delighted to report
　　That you became a hot pop property
　　When *Four Weddings* exhumed your poetry.
You would have been amused to see its star
Arrested with a hooker in his car

But shocked that we remain so schizophrenic.
　　Our sordid scandals rarely stay concealed
Although we want things guiltless and hygienic.
　　Gay Studies has developed as a field
　　In which great writers' lovers are revealed;
You lose some points for marrying a Mann
And your diversity of goings-on.

As your long-suffering but faithful fan,
　　I must disclose you missed the NEA,
The disco era, Gump and daily bran.
　　In short, you would assess the present day
　　As drearily debased and déclassé.
Well, Wystan, this is all that I can muster.
Give my regards to Byron.
　　　　　　　　　　　Fondly,
　　　　　　　　　　　Juster

# *First Confession*

Blood thudded in my ears. I scuffed,
  Steps stubborn, to the telltale booth
Beyond whose curtained portal coughed
  The robed repositor of truth.

The slat shot back. The universe
  Bowed down his cratered dome to hear
Enumerated my each curse,
  The sip snitched from my old man's beer,

My sloth pride envy lechery,
  The dime held back from Peter's Pence
With which I'd bribed my girl to pee
  That I might spy her instruments.

Hovering scale-pans when I'd done
  Settled their balance slow as silt
While in the restless dark I burned
  Bright as a brimstone in my guilt

Until as one feeds birds he doled
  Seven Our Fathers and a Hail
Which I to double-scrub my soul
  Intoned twice at the altar rail

Where Sunday in seraphic light
  I knelt, as full of grace as most,

## X. J. KENNEDY

And stuck my tongue out at the priest:
A fresh roost for the Holy Ghost.

# X. J. KENNEDY

## *Hangover Mass*

Of all sins of the flesh, that reprobate
  My father had but one, and it had class:
To sip tea of a Sunday till so late
  We'd barely make it up to Drunkards' Mass.

After a sermon on the wiles of booze,
  The bread and wine transformed with decent haste,
Quickly the priest would drive us forth to graze
  Where among churchyard flocks I'd get a taste

Of chronic loneliness. Red-rimmed of eye,
  Quaking of hand, old men my old man knew
Would congregate to help bad time go by:
  Stout Denny Casey, gaunt Dan Donahue

Who'd mention girls with withering contempt,
  Each man long gone past hope to meet his match
Unless in what he drank all night, or dreamt.
  Each knee I stared at cried out for a patch.

A sealed half-pint, I'd stand there keeping mum
  Till, bored to death, I'd throw a fit of shakes.
Then with relief we'd both go stepping home
  Over sidewalk cracks' imaginary snakes.

# X. J. KENNEDY

## *Theater of Dionysus*

*From* Inscriptions After Fact

*Athens, U. S. Sixth Fleet*

By the aisle on a stone bench
In the Theater of Dionysus
I make a flock of Greek kids smile
Sketching them Mickey Mouses

Where beery Aristophanes
By sanction till night's fall
Ribbed Eleusinian mysteries
With queer-joke and pratt-fall.

On high from the sacked Parthenon
A blackbird faintly warbles.
Sellers of paperweights resell
The Elgin marbles.

Here where queen-betrayed
Agamemnon had to don
Wine-purple robes, boys in torn drabs
Try my whitehat on,

Over stones where Orestes fled
The sonorous Furies
Girls hawking flyspecked postcards
Pursue the tourist.

# X. J. KENNEDY

Here in her anguish-mask
Andromache
Mourned her slain son — "Young man,
Aren't you from Schenectady?"

As I trudge down, a pebble breaks
Rattling across stone tiers,
Scattering echoes:  do I kick
A watcher's skull downstairs?

Silence imponders back
As I take the stage, the pebble
Stilled on a lower tier.
Trailing home now, the child rabble.

I stand in the center of the stage,
Could speak, but the sun's setting
In back of neon signs. Night unsheathes
Her chill blade. Better be getting

Back to the destroyer, radared bark,
No thresh of oars, sails with gods' crests —
Does the wind stir through the dark
Or does a throng of ghosts?

I run. Inaudible laughter drives
Offstage my spirit
As in the parched grass, wind routs
A white shiver before it.

## X. J. KENNEDY

# *One-Night Homecoming*

Opening the door, he grasps my suitcase handle,
But can't quite lift it. Breathes hard, mounting stairs.
She doesn't notice yolk stuck to the dishes,
Nailheads arising from the kitchen chairs.

*Where are the kids?* In school. *You didn't bring them?*
I'll be your kid, I say, but can't compete
With her persistent needling iteration
That hurts without intending to, like sleet.

From childhood's bed I follow in the ceiling
The latest progress of each crack I know,
But still the general cave-in hangs suspended,
Its capillary action running slow,

And the huge roof I used to think unchanging
Gives with each wind. It's my turn now to fall
Over strewn blocks, stuffed animals on staircases,
My turn to read the writing crayoned on the wall.

# *Ballade: 1985*

*Horribilis*, that *annus* was. A year
Of misbegotten days and nights I lost
All track of. Breakfast meant two cans of beer
Before my car could drive to work. It cost
Me more than I should say: a lover tossed
Away as if she were some Magdalen.
I *knew* that she was what I needed most.
I never want to live that way again.

I never want to wake up soaked in fear,
Not knowing if, the night before, I'd crossed
Someone who could have slit my life from ear
To ear, but hadn't, from contempt. From post
To pillar, from revilement to disgust,
In Fortune's eyes and in the eyes of men,
I drank to throw up on this party's host.
I never want to live that way again,

When every credit card was in arrears
And yet I thought that I was Robert Frost.
I never want to hear that man from Sears
Explain — at 10:00 p.m., when I am sauced —
What courts could do to me; or dream The Ghost
Of Visa Past Due knew me way back when
I'd sold my sober soul to play at Faust.
I never want to live that way again.

Instead, I'd rather live like this, and boast
To friends, "Well, this is now, and hell was then,
And at this moment I propose a toast:
'May no man need to live that way again.'"

## *Father/Shaving/Mirror*

Behind the bathroom door, I move as if
By rote, then stand, at last, before a glass
All fogged with steam — the shower's daily gift
That keeps me from my face. It comes to this

Each morning, but from here on in, I'll cut
Not just my own, but someone else's cheek:
That stubbled skin I kissed when I was eight.
Its beard is mine now. Now no longer sleek

With boyhood's smooth, untroubled flesh, my jaw
Seems firmly set against my father's blade.
Each day, the mirror's foamed façade, scraped raw
And red, comes clearer from its masquerade

As someone else. He's doubled now. We trade
Our places, rinse and slap and towel down.
Now twenty-eight, his age when I was made,
I razor off a frowning, lathered clown

Whose throat is his. Our Slavic jowls and cheeks,
Inflected by an upper lip too thin
For shaving safely, wreak their havoc: nicks
And cuts we've learned to take upon the chin.

The two of us, who share a dimple now,
A pair of laugh lines, one deep philtrum, meet

# LEN KRISAK

Each morning, paint like mimes, and like mimes, saw
With single, silent, simple steel. We greet

The day in one another, realize
Our more-than-homely task, and know for good,
We need not ask what's in each other's eyes,
For here is where I've drawn my only blood.

# *Baptistery*

Like God, these boxed-in stanzas will provide,
So what you read here is not merely pride
Re-doubled in another kind of space,
Another room, another testing place
For artist and for subject-sacrifice.
No. Here is faith; I trust it will suffice.
I trust that it will be as well re-paid
As I was for the sacrifice I made
Of Isaac and his father Abraham.
Ready for the story? I know I am.

I know *I Am* in all His glory, too.
How else have won what I was set to do?
He held my hand, and Brunelleschi lost,
So surely twenty years were worth the cost.
(That's what it took to execute these doors
In bronze, with gilt — while Florence waged its wars.)
I waged a campaign of my own, you see,
Laying siege to the judges — secretly —
For one whole year before we cast our trial
Pieces (that's how their style became my style).

— And how I knew that Isaac must be nude.
See how his chest and its exactitude
Of muscle, rib, and carven flesh confront
You? That's what you, the judges, and God want:
Naked obedience. The boy looks straight

Into his papa's eyes — and so his fate —
With dumb surprise. The father concentrates
Just like a knife point, lends the massive gates
Their subject: this is one way in to God.
His servant-priest declines to spare the rod.

Oblivious in killer love's intent,
This pillar does not see the ram that's meant
For holocaust. But caught in thorns, the beast
Awaits, behind, on rocks that I have creased
And crumpled like stiff paper. Blind as well
To how the angel bursts the sky to tell
Him no in just the nick of time, that man
Stands still, forever stopped — which was my plan.
The servants pose, unknowing, not a clue
To what is going to go on. And you?

Are you, at last, more caught up than that ram,
That ass? And who's the priest and who the lamb?
Where is *your* "leap of faith" who stop and stare,
Arrested by the moment frozen there?
Look hard and see how I have filled with toil,
With brazen drama, all this quatrefoil.
Consider what I've raised in bas-relief.
And can you hear the bleat and baa? Belief,
Beyond the doorway, summons and demands.
Come. Bathe your babes. Step through. The Lord commands.

# *Tantalus*

My fate is cruel? No doubt it makes you think
Of Dante, how I'm in it up to here.
The pool is warm, I tell myself; to drink
It wouldn't cool me anyway. No tear
Would be in order. And to eat the fruits
That hang above me on that long, lone branch
Would only lead to fouling what I stand
In. No, it's better this way. This way suits
Me fine, thank you. In water free of stench,
I contemplate one perfect apple wind
Would only blow away were I to reach.
Weep not for me, my gentle reader. Each
Man wants some thing by which his soul is teased
And taunted, learning how it will be pleased.

# LEN KRISAK

## *Skye*

*Translation of the Latin poem "Skia"*
*by Samuel Johnson*

The deepest seas embrace the Isle of Skye
  And give it height and place and form.
  Who sees its cliff walls blown with storm,
  And hears its rock-sown shores resound
With squalls, knows all that pleases ear and eye;
  He sees the cloud-white sky above each bay
  And cove, and loves what he has found.

And I believe with all my mortal heart
  That insofar as any man
  Can cure his soul, on Skye he can.
  For rage is banned from every site,
And grief's been made an exile from the start
  From this small isle. Peace practices its art
  Where quiet respite fears no spite.

I know that this is so, and yet . . . I know
  As well that hiding in the caves
  Of Skye, or counting starving waves
  From crags that carve sky like a prow,
Or climbing hills where nothing good will grow,
  And lonely humankind will never go,
  Is not enough. I know that now,

And tell you this:  that man cannot provide
Himself. He cannot make his own
Heart's peace from everything like stone
Inside it. Even in a place
Like Skye, his power has no force; his pride
Will not suffice. The school of Stoics lied
To teach he was his own true grace.

No, God the King — our greatest king — commands
In everything that stirs each part
Of man with storm. No human chart
Alone can tame those seas; the will
Of God shall have them surge when He demands.
And as He calms them by His loving hands,
The tempest of the soul lies still.

# *Abraham*

I praised the job my boy had done,
The fire he'd helped to build
For something not yet killed.
I doused the lamp, and watched him run

In mock fear, hoping he'd be caught.
A Sunday School exam
Once pictured Abraham,
Building a fire although they'd brought

No sheep or goat for sacrifice,
Isaac transfixed with fear
No offering tethered near,
No distant bleating, he the price

Paid God. For what? They knew no motive,
Unlike the reluctant slaughter
Of Agamemnon's daughter
At Aulis, whom the priest made votive

That the lord of men could sail, the Greek
Whose goddess held a grudge
Only his girl could budge
From its severe, Olympian peak.

These disembodied faces which
Illuminate our camp

I'd put out with the lamp,
But their glow doesn't have a switch.

# ANTHONY LOMBARDY

## *When Love Was Rome*

> *Did I not say, Prodike, we grow old*
> *That love's thick braid comes disentwined?*
> *Now sagging mouth, gray hair, and wrinkles rule*
> *The face your beauty has resigned.*
> — *Rufinus*

When love was Rome, and I a loyal knight,
I bore your assignations in the forum,
The scandal of lubricious indecorum,
The grand emotivism of your plight.
I was received by you and ever since
I've gathered taxes and the council quorum,
Still like a gift I've paid the ad valorem,
When love was Rome, and I a client prince.
But now that you have fallen out of favor,
And mighty Rome itself begins to fall,
I feel my loyalty begin to waver.
That age against which we had built our wall
Too savagely has vandalized us all
For us to save that Empire which we savor.

# ANTHONY LOMBARDY

## *A Letter Home*

They do not make it all that easy here
To know the city trains or how to wear
The latest look or decorate a store.

Tough luck if you're not smart and beautiful
And don't work hard in order not to fail
At that long-dreamt-of job in some hotel.

What virtues have they got? They're practical
And fast, they sweep the snow, deliver mail,
Get rid of trash, and keep the budget small,

The little girls are dressed without a patch
Each boy has got good sneakers and a watch,
And of the past no one remembers much.

The streets are what you've heard about before;
The noise is somewhat less than one can bear.
The beggars aren't as broke as they appear.

Somehow the institutions stand intact;
The church and modern art remain well liked
And no one's liberties have been revoked.

If you are young and looking there are lanes
And parks with lanterns like a hundred moons
And eyes that swim upon the flowing lawns.

# ANTHONY LOMBARDY

And if you are run over by a tram
Its bells will ring and one or two will come
To shake their heads and say it was a shame.

But, having written that, I feel ashamed
To suddenly regret the door I slammed
Upon the face this country has assumed,

Because I've listened to the breath and voice
Beyond my door, which tried but could not pass
Within my heart, whose latch I now release

At last to silence, to a caller gone
Already out into the mincing rain
Of this strange land where the virtues are our own.

# *Archilochus*

Count him unlucky both in life and love,
Whom girl and downcast shield accuse
Of shameful deeds, as with Archilochus,
Servant of Ares and the Muse.

Some think that history shows the greedy get
What they are after, while the good
Get lost; the lucky often think that luck
Follows virtue and that it should.

I think the wind on the Aegean shore
Knows neither good nor bad, but rates
The one whom it indifferently exalts
With him whom it humiliates.

Between my schoolbooks I would always bring
The D and the demerit slip.
While others struggled, somehow I both failed
The test and got the scholarship.

On Wall Street, having lost my job and hopes
Of earning what my father earned,
I won with bold, small poems the girl for whom
The brokers making it had yearned.

Impulsively I bought a farm, a deed
All cautions urged us not to do.

# ANTHONY LOMBARDY

I was the fool who'd emptied our accounts
Until they cut the highway through.

I do not have a heart of perfect faith.
But merely laziness and nerve.
I merit nothing of the luck I've had,
Unless to love is to deserve

The thing one loves, in which case I am not
So undeserving, and if some
Long overdue misfortune falls my way,
And I end up like that old bum,

I'd still be happy, like Archilochus,
Unlucky man, whose words professed
That he did not do well, but whose few lines
Are proof he did do what was best.

# *The Poet's Personality Test*

I'm told this mental profile can
reveal what lives inside a man,
and name the famous poet's heart
that beats within my public part.
If I'm my idol, Robert Frost,
whose praise, on me, is never lost,
I'll know, by transitivity,
that the living Robert Frost is me!
And if, perhaps, Lord Tennyson
has been the mumbling denizen
who drums my versifying breast,
one still could not dismiss the test
that knows a stately anapest!
And if I'm Nelson, (Marilyn),
I would not think, "Let's try again."
This old, white house could do far worse
than to be haunted by such verse!
I click the answers, punch "return,"
and am perplexed at what I learn:
that I'm not bitter, not bound to fail,
not cynical, and not a male!
Before today I never knew
that I was Maya Angelou!
This revelation takes my breath,
but I can see that after death,
when Peter asks me who I am
I might just wink and work a scam,

# ANTHONY LOMBARDY

there where gender has no glory
and race is not a category,
especially since my own good name
is not of angels nor of fame,
and the choirs there seem a little weak
on niceties of verse technique.
Assuming that I get there first,
my story will be well rehearsed:
I'll rattle loudly at the gate,
lest the apostle hesitate
to turn the key and let me through
to be the woman all men knew
as the laureled Maya Angelou!

# Love Song

*We have lingered in the chambers of the sea*
*By sea-girls wreathed with seaweed red and brown*
*Till human voices wake us . . .*

*"Prufrock"*

The new pier is concrete, the streets are paved.
The surfers wear short hair — nothing's been saved
Since you were last here, an epoch ago.
Everyone's faster and thinner than you,
The glassy bodies, ageless, browned, and bleached.

Most stands have changed, but the food still tastes of brine.
And the shore is constant, the day plays on without time.
The games remain, world-class and record-breaking:
A sleek-muscled young man digs and dives and spikes.
The crowd shrieks and shouts his name: "Troy! Troy!"

So once you thought you governed this beach . . .
Now, twice the age of girls catching you stare.
Surprised to find the sudden urge still there,
You glance away and study partial shells. . . .
And imagine you'd still be received well.

You'd leave your life for the Filipina on skates,
Whose long black hair shines like copper in the sun.
It falls on her back to a perfect "v,"

Pointing to the cleft showing above her bikini.
She circles and smiles past you, smelling of lemons.

Down coast a Latina — or southern European —
Knows you're looking and shifts her hips in the sand.
She slowly smoothes lotion on her almond thighs,
Frowning in a glamorous pose she's gleaned
From the perfumed pages of her magazine.

You'll speak with that blonde, just now parting her legs
To better paint her toenails pink.
She unties her shoulder strings to tan —
What will you say? Your hair matches her zebraskin mat?
You hadn't seen her tall boyfriend playing catch.

Is your stroll over? Is it getting dark?
You've had this afternoon to your old self.
Late boats sail toward port, a family lights a fire and sings.
Your wife is waiting to nurse the baby.
They, too, mock your time and lead back home.

## *Projections*

A sudden gift arrives from Mother, wrapped
"Boutique-Exact," the label says, with bows
And velvet paper, black. It's far from Christmas;
My birthday's passed. Yet Mother's sending clothes —
A way of mending us. We can't discuss
My life these days without my feeling trapped

In marriage or embarrassed that hubby's lame.
He doesn't work as hard around the house
As others do, she notices. But he's
Content to stay in place and won't carouse
(As others do) at every opportunity.
Besides, was Daddy any *crème de la crème?*

His frequent meetings often took all night.
He napped each afternoon. Our quiet play
Disturbed him anyway: the bedspread strewn,
His brow wet — restless signs his dreams betrayed.
He'd rouse upset, then leave as though immune
From duty. Mornings after, they would fight.

Twelve years, they never learned to reconcile.
We saw their breaking up before they did,
And found no answers in their gifts to us. . . .

As now, another hint to have a child: a grid
Of silky strings and matching stockings, useless
Advice from one who wore too late this style.

# From the Notebooks of Count Galeazzo Ciano

*October 1942*

The light wines he offered in the parlor
Of his Roman headquarters in the palace,
The Belgian chestnuts and brandied coffee,
All talk of politics finished for the night.
We moved at leisure about the large rooms,
Viewing the terrible art he commissioned —

Portraits of himself in furious pose,
Mostly, leading his high-stepping legions
Or standing erect before the red flag,
His stiff arm correct in peculiar salute.
This arrogant Austrian of common stock!

Imagine his speaking of the sublime!
How the Italians were too passionate
To make the Renaissance more than Beauty!
"Art must depict the world's direction, *Conte*,
Not merely show us its spirit and time."

How dare he address me in cultured tones,
Among shadows of his image, massive bronzed busts
Lining the front corridor, his warring brow
Dunning the few Masters allowed to remain.

No matter. They will outlast all tyrants
And countries, the Masters — even the Axis
Crushing beneath the blacking of his boot.

Indulge this monster for Italia's good?
Pompeii still displays the worthy governance
Of paintings and urns, statues and visages . . .
Enduring beyond the great triumvirate.

## *Pilate*

O civil Rome! Let me command legions
Across new lands once more, conquer nations
And return home, marching triumphantly!
I've not the conscience for diplomacy.

My wife wakens, terrified by a dream.
I count the long days left to my regime
Among these fickle, nomadic people.
Young Jesus pledged to them life eternal —
They want him dead to prove he's not their god.

But who should decide? I? They, or Herod?
The issue is political desire —
Theirs and mine — not crime against the Empire.
Whether or not they are allowed to choose
To free Barabbas or this "king" of Jews,
Rome cannot yield responsibility.

Alone having the power to decree
The death of any man or miracle
And to render prophecies practical,
Rome fulfills all laws. Gods are made by us . . .
And we're to make another of Jesus;
Of victim, rule. Too late the countermands,
Of this matter I wash my knowing hands.

## The Paintings of Arnesti Gaspári

"It can't be done! The visage I wanted
On canvas, each detailed light in my mind,
And the misguided distortions I find
Drying before me — death, consecrated
Failing, mutations from *my* hand? Dreaded
Soul of no worth but this surreal slime!
Guido will pleasure to mock me in kind,
Filth-monger, his greedy eyes alerted
Only to gold, the scab, commercial worm.

"Yet he works daily, and his unworthy,
Stolen images sell. When will I learn?
My early dungeon pieces — let's carry
Them to Vesta's fiery mouth. So shall burn
The paintings of Arnesti Gaspári!"

# CHARLES MARTIN

## *Lot's Wife Looks Back*

> *But Lot's wife behind him looked back,*
> *and she became a pillar of salt.*
> — Genesis 19:26

I want it told correctly from the first:
I was responsible, I had been warned,
And yet, in spite of knowing what I durst
Not do, from sheer perversity I turned,
Though not to see what there was left to see,
Which by that time was a mere pile of rubble
That held no further interest for me,
But just to make unprecedented trouble
(Not all that difficult back then), lest guile
And double-dealing fall into neglect,
And disobedience go out of style.
I did it then, for *me*, in retrospect,
And not from any inadvertency
Or out of misplaced sympathy for *them*:
Those cities of the plain were much too fancy
For His Omnipotence not to condemn.
When tourists asked me why I'd turned, I'd say
I had no choice, since I was picked by Lot;
That lost its humor when Lot passed away.
My turning back *did* complicate the plot,
Though it was certainly not *my* intention
That everything I thought or felt or knew
Should be salt-cured by divine intervention —

I was allowed my little joke or two,
But silenced otherwise. Not one more word.
Ages rolled by without another word from
The nameless wife of Lot — until the Lord
Fell silent too. These days He's unheard from,
Though not unheard *of*: the fame outlasts the act
And lives on in the collective memory
Past usefulness. Now, someone with less tact
Might argue that the same is true of me,
Though as Fates go, mine seems less disagreeable,
Providing that it doesn't last forever;
I want it known that, here, for the foreseeable
Future, I plan to stay, exuding savor.

# CHARLES MARTIN

## *Neither Here nor There*

*From* A Walk in the Hills above the Artists' House

### 1/

Late afternoon:  in studios
Where work is done or unbegun,
Disoriented poets close
The books on rough draft or revision;
Outside, as a declining sun
Takes aim at the Pacific Ocean,
A little clearing slowly fills
With those who'd like to walk the hills

### 2/

Above the temporary quarters
(Emptying out now for the hike)
Where composers, artists, writers
Have settled in to make their mark,
Each different but all alike
In having gotten time to work
As much or little as we please,
And walk sometime among the trees —

### 3/

Perhaps the same trees I flew over
After I managed to exchange
My sweaty feedbag for the clover
Of a few weeks' idleness;

# CHARLES MARTIN

Significant others find it strange,
But work that any artist does
Paradoxically depends
On leisure to achieve its ends.

### 4/

So here I am in my new cell,
Which might belong to anyone;
There's little that it has to tell
About the others who've passed through:
Wisps of patchouli linger on,
But no more urgent residue
Of effort, concentration, doubt —
No marks gouged in, no butts ground out,

### 5/

No sign of work brought to conclusion
By any former resident
Or left to trail off in confusion. . . .
A womb in which *I* may conceive,
Supportive yet indifferent,
It will recover when I leave,
And someone else, when I'm *not* here —
But wait a moment! I just got here:

### 6/

A week ago, in some suspense,
I'd driven up a golden coast
Past signs that threatened ARMED RESPONSE,
Straining my rent-a-wreck until —
*Have I gone past it? Am I lost?*

# CHARLES MARTIN

— A grand museum on a hill
Presented itself:  with the view
I caught a glimpse of *déjà vu*:

### 7/

My eyes if not my legs had been
(How did I know it?) here before:
A gate, a guard who let me in
To find the underground garage:
An elevator rose one floor
And opened up on a mirage;
I knew the place — and stood amazed
At the great villa Piso raised!

### 8/

Piso, the Getty of his time
(Both men had made it big in oil),
Who built at Herculaneum
A summer refuge from the dreary
Round of urban stress and toil,
His *Villa dei — Che? Papiri!*
The name applied to it much later
By an Italian excavator,

### 9/

Who found the room where Philodemus,
Philosopher in minor key,
Elaborated his great theme
In essay and in epigram;
Praised the mysterious faculty
For which he had no proper name:

Imagination, understood
As any art's supremest good.

10/
Vesuvius cried, "Hold that thought!"
And all his wit and eloquence,
Unread, unheard of, lay unsought;
Oblivion's new underground
Poet and scholar in residence
(Alas!) was nowhere to be found,
Until a pickaxe let in light
On notions long kept out of sight:

11/
Leaves of his Book, reduced to ash
And shoveled from a cluttered shelf,
Were almost thrown out with the trash:
"Oh — were those *scrolls*?" Now blackened lace.
At first uncertain of itself,
Each inkstained fragment finds a place;
There are few guides for the perplexed
When charred briquets become a text,

12/
And text becomes a voice that lifts
Off from its backing to present
Us with long-unaccustomed gifts;
Here Philodemus criticizes
Artists who merely represent,
Then asks a question that surprises:

"Why can't a painter paint instead
A man with, say, a horse's head?

13/
"Why can't he show us, if he wishes,
A human face upon a creature
With a tail just like a fish's?
Why must an artist be confined
To drawing images from nature,
Ignoring those that spring from mind?"
So, in a cell provided him
By Piso's will or Piso's whim,

14/
The poet artfully composed
In well-funded isolation;
Who did not own himself, proposed
The right of artists to create,
Each from his own imagination,
Rather than merely imitate;
"For, as we grasp in our dreams,
The world is hardly what it seems.

15/
"As our poets all inform us,
In poetry false may be true,
Great may be small, and small, enormous;
The fabulous is natural:
Cyclops complaining of the view
And Venus on her scallop shell
May have originated in a
Cheese that Piso served at dinner."

16/
Poets had little, Piso, plenty;
He loved the prestige that accrued
To him among the cognoscenti
Who fattened on his patronage;
How could his mansion *not* include
A room for his residing sage?
As well as one for pinky rings
And for the girlfriends' slinky things.

17/
The villa Piso built was soon
Unfit for *any* occupant;
It disappeared one afternoon
Under a flow of laval silt
That hardened into adamant.
I walked through one that had been built
In imitation of its plan
By a wealthy Californian,

18/
Then drove to the artists' colony
Much farther north — the inspiration
Of a modern mage whose alchemy
Resulted in *la pilule d'or*,
Which helped free sex from generation,
And made a large non-profit for
The foundation on whose real estate
I am ensconced now to create.

# CHARLES MARTIN

### 19/

And where, last night, we met our host,
Who did his best to break the ice
Between the salad and the roast:
"It seems to me the life you chose
Is a continual sacrifice
That you've accepted; yet, suppose
The work you did could find no venue —
Would you be willing to continue

### 20/

"If you could have no hope of any
Response from anyone at all,
Have neither fame nor love nor money,
Nor yet the thumbscrew nor the rack,
And — this, I think, would most appall —
Even indifference held back;
Given a worst-case scenario
Out of Beckett, Kafka, Poe —

### 21/

"Immured in some grim *oubliette*
Whence word of you would never issue,
And none there were who would regret
Your absence from the banquet table,
Or call you up to say, 'We miss you!'
Is it — I mean — would you be able,
Could you create, without the sense
Your work had use or consequence?"

22/

Good question. Once a poet-friend
Told me that if he ever heard
The world was coming to an end —
The missile launched with his name on it —
He'd try to put in a last word
Or two on an unfinished sonnet.
Although I think that I would try to
Find someone to say good-bye to,

23/

It is a personal decision
As to whether, at closing time,
The life or work most wants revision —
I can't do other than admire
His quest for one last, perfect rhyme,
Such a fierce refining fire —
I guess I ought to make it clear
I mean the poet's fire, here —

24/

But if our writing matters, what
Makes it matter matters more
Than *it* does — what goes on without,
In inexpressively tremendous
Regions of after and before
And happening right now, beyond us —
All that we simply do not get.
It promises us nothing, yet

# CHARLES MARTIN

25/

My poet-friend would have in mind
A saving grace to end up with,
As I would too — I'd hope to find
An image suitably oblique:
*The unilluminated moth*
*That fluttered from an opened book*
*And struggles to ascend on air*
*Will soon be neither here nor there.*

**DAVID MASON**

---

## *The Pond*

Downcast thermometers record one truth
of winter, though the clear light hints of spring.
The furnace blows a warming reverie
where I drop anchor somewhere in the woods
with a girl I haven't seen for twenty years.

I find the pond secluded in the park,
filled by a waterfall beside a bluff
where we held hands and jumped, yelling love,
laughing to find ourselves alive again
and young as always, touching each other's skin.

Tonight the temperature is due to fall,
an arctic stillness settle on the prairies . . .
The years slow down and look about for shelter
far from forests and far from summer ponds:
the mind ghosting out in a shoal of stars.

# *Letter to No Address*

Another winter holds the town at bay,
inward-looking as the river freezes,
dark water glazes over, and closes.
Home from work, I mark the narrowing day.

For hours this letter weighed upon my mind,
a secret hauled from underneath the ice,
kept from others till I could find a space
for lines I have no notion how to send.

The past I would recapture is a land
whose contours changed the further I moved out,
years from cedars where we built a hidden fort
and you were the scrappy leader of our band.

Brother, I want to map the old hardscrabble
places we ransacked, bluffs or high above,
leaping from stone to stone with a wild love,
the ache of play erasing all our trouble.

As boys we followed parents up the pass,
switchbacking marmot rocks through Devil's Club.
We hunkered under peaks from the weather's stab,
but storms could not prepare us for divorce.

That route, chosen without our consent,
abandoned children in a wilderness

where breaking voices met hard silences,
fear the one emotion never spent.

Perhaps to conquer fear, I followed you,
the distant older brother, when you traveled.
Like you I married, though my love unraveled
far from the woods and mountains that we knew.

And you were not a boy on that last climb.
The trouble you carried upward was your own,
The glacier where you fell as white as bone.
When I recall that instant I go numb.

I live in a world too full of elegies,
and find no compensation in these lines,
nor can they map where memory begins
its restoration under winter skies.

# Agnostos Topos

We had walked a whole day on high ridges
somewhere between the heat-struck sea and peaks,
each breath a desert in a traveler's lungs,
salt-stung, dusty, like summer's rasping grass
and the roughness of stone. Biblical thorns
penned us, while the stunted ilex trees
shadowed the path. It seemed from these dour fields
we could not emerge on anything like a road.

A landscape no one had commodified
or fenced. If there were gardens here
the poverty of soil defeated them.
If there were homes beyond some goatherd's hut
the gravity of ages pulled them down.
No sound but cicadas like high-pitched drills
ringing till red sunlight hissed into the sea.

And that was when, our shins scratched and throats parched,
we stumbled into a village on the shore
where people, stupefied by days upon days
that were the same, told us what to call this place.
The distance to a road? *Two cigarettes*,
said the old man who sat webbing his net.

Now the road cuts down from the cliffs above.
I've been back, bought wine from the old man's son
who keeps his car parked in an olive's shade.

It's better, of course, that one can come and go.
One needn't stare a lifetime at hot cliffs,
thinking them impassable except to goats
and men whose speech and features grew like thorns.

The old man's dead. The friends I traveled with
are long since out of touch, and I'll admit
I've lost much of a young man's nimbleness.
I call these passing years *agnostos topos*,
unknown country, a place of panting lizards.
Yet how like home it seemed when I walked down
out of the unfenced hills, thirsty, footsore,
with words of greeting for the fisherman.

**JOSHUA MEHIGAN**

## *A Cellar in Pankow*

*March 1945*

We stay put. From between two hollow halves,
as if it were a Russian doll, our future
egests, each day, a humbler miniature.
We catch ourselves believing this routine.
Spring, summer, fall, and winter: Two each, now,
divide us from our son, six months a Briton.
We share our cordial hosts' good graces, rations,
water, a view, this cellar, consolation.
I have become nearsighted. Isaac, too.
Then, like a picture one might someday enter,
this window, our inevitable view:
automobiles moving blackly through;
the faceless drivers' forward stare; then, closer,
under the ever-damp gray walls of neighbors
invisible to us but often heard,
big, melting sprays of bowed forsythia.
What would one peeking in at us observe?
Stunted life. Life that flows in conduits
of darkened, undiscovered shipwreck hulls.
But maybe also something of himself:
highlight and shadow, thin as his exhalations
dissolving on mid-March, or late November,
or January air. And then one day,
should we continue rising in this way,
madness or death. Forgive the lucky ones

their monumental, necessary crime.
For "it shall not come nigh thee." Or so says
another Jew who fought the Philistines.

## JOSHUA MEHIGAN

# *In the Home of My Sitter*

Mrs. Duane Krauss, sure of her solitude,
grimaced between the kitchen alcove's cryptic
lesser motifs of Elvis and Saint Jude,
herself the central subject of the triptych:
her young-old country cheeks and looming bust,
the timely smile, gathered around a lie.
She called me "dear," she bowed, she briefly fussed,
then turned to pat her mother's china dry.

I did my part. I showed how bright I was,
how self-assured. But I lacked common sense.
Even the dogs there knew — and not because
she humbled them with cozy sentiments —
that friends, not being family, not quite,
keep out of trouble and keep out of sight.

. . .

Across the white hill swallows fanned and scattered,
drawing my eye along till I could see
atop the hill — tilted and mossy, flattered
by early sun — an old barn, tempting me.
Morning to suppertime not much else mattered.
They must've known. I wanted them to know.
Morning to suppertime their still den chattered
with *Meet the Press* and Christian radio.

Patient, I watched the barn's roof simplify
to silhouette, and the hillside's azure glow
pass, as the night returned my errant eye,
to static white, the white of moonlit snow,
while those four faces I've not seen again
kept to the borrowed twilight of the den.

. . .

One face there, bright as ripening persimmon,
still a bit bitter, seldom looked at me:
that quiet *Vater* stooped amid his women,
who let his lenses flash for privacy.
High in the shadow of a naked rafter,
his stuffed barn owl outspread its furious wings,
a household daemon to discourage laughter,
unnecessary talk, and touching things.

. . .

Mother, my young, my beautiful rescuer! —
so late, so long, I might be waiting still,
my pure heart wondering always where you were,
if not for those four strangers on their hill,
who, loath to form a fair impression of me,
simply did not, as you must always, love me.

## JOSHUA MEHIGAN

# *Schism by Twilight*

From where we fought at sunset on the pier,
that huge ungraspable perplexity
of power and motion, light and atmosphere,
could seem to you a token surety,

as if the never-ending blue veneer
and high shell-colored mares' tails we could see
were images to have and to hold dear,
daubed on a jewelry box, but feelingly,

an heirloom of our human family,
but tendered with a smile to us two here:
to brighten all life's rainy subtlety,
console me on my way, and help me bear

my mind, as yours has been borne year by year,
from will to shall, in Cosmic Harmony.

# *Alexandra*

*"A man was distressed in mind because of me. . . .*
*I chose to betake myself alive into the tomb."*

For ten years I have known
only this shadow-show
that interrupts the glow
cast on my walls of stone.
I've felt my innocence.
Shifting to bask in it,
I've often found it lit
a darker consequence.

Bright mornings promise spring.
I used to wish for birds,
for music stripped of words.
It comes: fierce, echoing,
strange as the specks of gray
that on the sunlight's dumb,
slow, fluid medium
soar mercifully away.

This evening, stirred by fear,
I looked out at the weather
and spied two forms together.
Did they spy me in here?
Wouldn't they laugh to see
themselves as I must: shades

fading, as twilight fades,
inconsequentially?

My walls are interlaced
with waving shapes, all slight,
all, slowly as the light,
passing like parceled waste.
In the sandy glow
on these walls of stone
I may yet be shown
all I need to know.

# JOSHUA MEHIGAN

## *Merrily*

> *"And we sleep all the way; from the womb to the grave*
> *we are never thoroughly awake; but passe on with such*
> *dreames, and imaginations as these . . ."*
>
> — *John Donne*

If only their significance were clear.
This quick, green bank. The sun's autistic eye,
oblivious to one more pioneer.
Unmeaning blue, less sky than anti-sky.
West, through the trees' meshed crowns, light scattering
toward such specific ends! Why those? And why
these flexed roots? Why that oak's failed rendering
of coupled elephants in living wood?
Its leaves smell sour, although it feels like spring.
I could go on. *Quis homo?* It's no good:
The more things blur, the clearer I become.
I could go on forever if I could.
Meanwhile, my boat moves downstream, listing some.
The question tails away. Against the prow
pumped gently by the surge, my back goes numb.
Behind, a riot-swept feather or split bough
neither recedes nor gains. As if to steer,
I drop a hand in. Oh, well. Anyhow,
the scenery is mesmerizing here.

## ROBERT MEZEY

# *A Coffee House Lecture*

Come now, you who carry
  Your passions on your back,
Will insolence and envy
  Get you the skill you lack?
Scorning the lonely hours
  That other men have spent,
How can you hope to fathom
  What made them eloquent?

Blake tells you in his notebooks,
  If you would understand,
That Style and Execution
  Are Feeling's only friend,
That all Poetic Wisdom
  Begins in the minute,
And Vision sees most clearly
  While fingering a lute.

Robert Burns in Ayreshire
  With meter and with gauge
Studied the strict exactitudes
  That illuminate his page,
Ignored the vulgar grandeur
  That you and yours hold dear,
And labored with his body
  And his perfected ear.

# ROBERT MEZEY

Valéry gripped a scalpel
And sweated at his task,
Bent over bleeding Chaos
In spotless gown and mask;
And in reluctant lectures
Spoke of the cruel art
And cold precise transactions
That warm the human heart.

How many that have toiled
At the hard craft of verse
Had nothing more than music
To fill their empty purse,
But found it was sufficient
In making out a will
To pay for their mortality,
And they are living still.

# ROBERT MEZEY

## *A Note She Might Have Left*

Sorry I couldn't give you the details
       or say goodbye;
   but if you feel beguiled,
it was your nature to turn a blind eye.
Only children believe in fairy tales
       and you're a child.
   And everything you had me say
      I said in play.

The play is over now, but still you stand
       on the empty stage
   where the great loves live on,
crying out to the darkness in a rage
that only the two actors understand.
       But one is gone,
   and all her speech was meaningless.
      So was the kiss.

# ROBERT MEZEY

## *No Country You Remember*

But for the steady wash of rain,
The house is quiet now. Outside,
An occasional car moves past the lawn
And leaves the stillness purified.

I find myself in a dark chair
Idly picking a banjo, lost
In reveries of another time,
Thinking at what heavy cost

I came to this particular place,
This house in which I let my life
Play out its subterranean plot,
My Christian and enduring wife.

What if I paid for what I got?
Nothing can so exhaust the heart
As boredom and self-loathing do,
Which are the poisons of my art.

All day I resurrect the past.
This instrument I love so ill
Hammers and rings and, when I wish,
Lies in its coffin and is still.

I dream of winter mornings when
Between bare woods and a wrecked shack

# ROBERT MEZEY

I came down deep encrusted slopes,
A bag of dead birds at my back,

Then let my mind go blank and smile
For what small game the mind demands,
As dead time flickers in the blind
Articulation of my hands.

I know you must despise me, you
Who judge and measure everything
And live by little absolutes —
What would you like to hear me sing?

A strophe on the wasted life?
Some verses dealing with my fall?
Or would you care to contemplate
My contemplation of the wall?

I write from down here, where I live.
In the cold light of a dying day,
The covered page looks cold and dead.
And — what more is there to say

Except, you read this in a dream.
I wrote nothing. I sat and ate
Some frozen dinner while I watched
The Late Show, and the Late Late.

# ROBERT MEZEY

## *Back*

Tonight I looked at the pale northern sky
Above the city lights, and both the stars
And the lamps of men faded and burned by turns,
Breathed in and out. You would have liked it here,
The emptiness, the wind across the fields,
And the spring coming on — especially
The strange white almond blossoms, their unfolding
When a car swings down the lane towards the orchard
And turns its headlights on them. Hard as it was,
I forced myself to think of everything
You liked best, the years before you died
In a locked room in an army hospital.
Or was it after that, in a southern city,
Watching the traffic lights go on and off
And the big-finned cars swim past in a blur of rain?
I know your heart stopped once when, slightly drunk,
Holding your daughter's hand, you stood before
The cage of a small, shuddering European bear.
That spring in Half Moon Bay, where the sad surf
Felt up and down the beach with endless sighs,
And in the morning the brown seaweed lay
Like old surgical tubing. It could have been
Any one of a hundred times and places.
But last night, opening your eyes from sleep
To the steady courtyard light, I heard your breath
Coming and going like a wounded thing
That would not die. It could have been
Nothing but mine, persisting one more night.

**ROBERT MEZEY**

## *After Ten Years*

*after Borges*

Now that the sum of footsteps given you
to walk upon the earth has been fulfilled,
I say that you have died. I too have died.
I, who recall the very night we made
our laughing, unaware farewells, I wonder
what on earth has become of those two young men
who sometime around 1957
would walk for hours, oblivious of the snow
that slashed around those street corners like knives
under the lamps of that midwestern town,
or sit in bars, talking about the women,
or decades later, stroll the perfumed streets
of Pasadena, talking about the meters.
Brother in the felicities of the Herberts,
George and Zbigniew, and of Chivas Regal,
and the warm rooms of the pentameter,
discoverer, as we all were in those days,
of that timeworn utensil, metaphor,
Henri, my tipsy, diffident old friend,
if only you were here to share with me
this empty dusk, however impossibly,
and help me to improve these lines of verse.

# *The Sunday School Lesson*

*north Louisiana*

The room was full of thirteen-year-old boys
Unhappily constrained by polished shoes,
Bow ties, oiled hair, orders against all noise,
And one eternal hour of Good News.

I joined the class each summer in July
When visiting my kin in that small town,
Lazing away the weeks till by and by
The signs of autumn brought my parents down.

Distracted like the rest, I, too, was bored
Though not a friend who shared the cycling year's
High rites of church, school, fair, and sports that stored
A common mind with common loves and fears.

Long-legged and ungainly in my chair,
I'd lean on the shoved-up window while the fan
Would spin a weightless haze of heated air
Around the sullen room as class began.

Jack Hopkins was our teacher though I doubt
He ever saw himself as any more
Than someone who could see an hour out
With tall tales of his catch the night before.

# DAVID MIDDLETON

I'd watch his bulbous nose and long-drawn face
Both reddened in a steady heart's decline
As once more he would tell, with skill and grace,
Of nine-pound bass caught on a two-pound line.

One day, though, he seemed different, hardly there,
Gazing over the graves with restless eyes,
Searching for something distant and yet near,
Unfixable in cloudless summer skies.

At last, he slowly read, then half-recited
In a strong drawl which measured out King James,
Those passages in Matthew where affrighted
Disciples cried to Jesus as He came

Walking across night's foam upon the water
To grasp weakening Peter who'd looked down,
Distracted by the winds that made him totter,
Now mastered by the fear that he would drown.

Fumbling with his glasses, Mr. Jack then tried
With chuckles and an animated glance
Around a room from which all sound had died
To end the solemn calm and his own trance.

Those verses always moved him, he confessed,
Because of that strange evening on the lake
When a sudden storm caught him and he pressed
Against its wind to reach a cypress brake.

Perhaps it was the play of dark and light
Or just his tiredness vivified with fear,
And yet he swore that at the torrent's height
He saw the Christ by lightning drawing near.

With that, the lesson ended and the class
Rose awkwardly one by one and left the room
Embarrassed, even scared to have to pass
This man who'd gazed beyond the body's doom.

And though time brought him soon to what he saw,
It took me over thirty years to know
How soul's redeemed by wonder, lost in awe
Before those depths through which I, too, must go

With doubt and faith like Peter on the sea
Sinking in fear and chaos of the foam
Yet looking up toward one who has to be
There before the winds to take us home.

# DAVID MIDDLETON

## *A Quiet Reply*

*For my mother, Anna Sudduth Middleton,*
*who became a housewife and mother*
*in the 1940s in north Louisiana*

The house is silent now, yet through the rooms
Once filled with laughter, music, talk, and tears
I hear the sounds of children who will play
As long as love still draws their spirits near.
And there beside a window what remains
Of my good husband stares across the yard
At that locked greenhouse he cannot recall
Ever having built or even seen before.
His pension, savings, what the children send
Will do until he dies and I move in
With one of them to live in that last room
With pictures and the pictures in my mind.
A housewife and a mother who performed
The common sacraments of daily life
On stove and tabletop and ironing board,
I thought my work a calling, nothing less.
My sons' wives seem to think me incomplete
Yet there they are, outraged by their own tears
When toddlers left at day-care cling and scream
Torn from their mothers' arms before the dawn
And not picked up till dusk by those who gave
Their best at work and now crave rest alone.
I hold my tongue and let its quiet reply

Be answer to their barely hidden guilt
That would in me have cried out from the heart
Where deepest things can never be denied.
But still I pause and try to understand
The kind of lives they say they have to live
And wonder whether I am one of those
Whose bent was taken late from ancient ways
Now passing with the world I used to know.

And yet I still remember and remain
In that sweet peace I entered long ago
Trusting in those old customs love sustains
By sacrifice till truth is realized.
Our wedding night on which we gave ourselves
As virgins to the ways of man and wife,
Those early months before the children came,
That small garage apartment where we lived
On what a navy seaman was allowed,
Then parenthood that bonded us in joy
And duty to the family and to God —
Such blessings were the laws that set me free
Through all those years the children were at home —
Nursing them with milk from my own heavy breasts,
Coming to calm their night fears with a hug,
Watching them sleep and wake, helping them walk,
Reading them Bible stories, Mother Goose,
Teaching them colors, numbers, shapes, and words,
And showing them the games I used to play,
Ring-around-the-roses, hopscotch, hide-and-seek.
And for my love of them, my husband, too,
I made a home for us as best I could

# DAVID MIDDLETON

And welcomed every task I had to do,
Washing the breakfast dishes, folding clothes,
Cleaning the house or going to the store,
Gardening and sewing, working at church,
Absorbed in the sacred making of the day.
Thanksgiving, Christmas, Easter, summertime,
The births and birthdays, marriages and deaths —
These were the greater and the lesser feasts
That filled life's calendar with poignancies.

The children now of course are grown and gone,
My husband only waiting, tired of life,
My days with him but disciplined routines
Of food and drugs, of silences and naps,
Then bed in which each struggling breath sustains
A body all but ready for its death.
I know he soon will pass away and I
Will leave this house in which for fifty years
We found our place within a settled world
Where God permits us all to apprehend
The nature of creation and its end.
And what will I remember when I go
To live my final years in that last room
One of my children must prepare for me?
The night I showed my husband our firstborn
Was kicking in the womb I made him press,
The first warm cup of tea those autumn dawns
I relished in the coolness on the porch
Before my family woke, or that quiet day
I told my youngest child about the time
The sun stood still for Joshua while outside

That very sun at noon shone down again
On irises that seemed to bloom and bloom
Forever in those lingering full beams
Until our eyes grew bright with selfless love.
Such moments stay alive within my heart
And in this private journal where for years
I've filled so many pages, not with rage,
But love preserved in memory's glad tears.

# DAVID MIDDLETON

## *The Craft of Noah*

*From* The Middle World

In clearest day, in clearest blue of noon,
Out of the brightest clarity of the sky,
As I rested there beside the olive fields
I heard my name repeated by the Lord
In an almond's cloud-white bough, and I awoke,
As if from sleep, beneath the leafless tree.
He spoke to His own reason, fixed in me,
Of mysteries beyond the reason's end,
Enabling thus by my contracted craft
A hidden revelation of His means.
So, in cloudless spring, amid the withered dill,
I built of driest cypress caulked with tar
An ark some fifty cubits straight across,
Three hundred cubits long and thirty deep
Raised up on bracing stands, as He decreed.
And there, when men made brutish by their vice
Hooted my work of curious design
Fashioned by tools from Adam handed down,
I pitched my voice across a fading sky
Calling from night by names they hardly knew
The beings of creation, two by two.
They came aboard as raindrops splattered the planks,
The wrinkled elephants ponderous and slow
And darted dragonflies so quickly still,
Mammals, amphibians, reptiles, insects, birds,

The animal kingdom ordered by His will!
And where the closest breeds remained discrete,
The godwit and the whimbrel well defined,
I saw the ghostly species take their place,
Those unmade shapes who prove the world divine.
Then, when my sons and daughters entered the ship
And looked down on the damned wading hard at last
To clutch at the holy thing I made of wood,
There poured from the broken heavens and the land
Foam of Chaos lifting us up over
The surfacing depths out of the world of man.
Thus I, the chosen witness of the scene,
Watched the rain of justice cover the earth,
A saltless sea where salt tears shed too late
By those long sunk in gluttony and lust
Embittered the tide that swept them from the peaks
And flooded the ruins of Eden with their blood,
While guided by my craft, this starward ark,
I rose on the trembling image of the dark.

# DAVID MIDDLETON

## *The Naming of the Trees: Odysseus to Laertes*

Od. *XXIV*

Old man, whoever you are, serf or king,
Who wrested out of nature this orchard
Kept by labor and the favor of the gods,
Dust off your knees, get up out of the soil,
And sit by this tall tree you surely planted:
I am a royal stranger, hear my tale!

I fought with Agamemnon ten long years
Before the holy citadel of Troy.
I was the first to grasp Odysseus' mind
And gladly hacked down firs to rib that horse
The pious Trojans thought no hollow gift
Though Zeus by then had given them to us.

That night they got a bellyful of Greeks
And woke to armies entering opened gates
Butchering the royals in their sleep,
Aeneas alone eluding us through flames
In which restrained Apollo, looking on, saw
The blood of Priam bubbling on the stones.

For ten years after that I wandered toward home
Strangely tangled in woodcraft, herbs, and trees —
Gardens of Alcinous, the poplar raft,

White moly and the Cyclops' shafted eye —
Still haunted by the image of a horse
Made to seem a thing it could not be.

At last I happened to land upon this isle —
Ithaca, is it not? — and saw in these
Green terraces and fields the vast plantations
Of an absent king. I found his palace
Held by feculent men. I slaughtered them all,
Then came to give you proof of who I am.

Here in this tended orchard grow trees
Whose names the young Odysseus learned to say
Numbering each kind planted in its row.
Over there stand ten apples whose round rough trunks
Brushed by the soft spring leaves and pinkish blooms
Are weighed down in fall by reddened pomes.

Then spaced out in the open forty figs
With broad leaves deeply lobed take the full sun
Bronzing their oblong globes of sweetest flesh.
Near them, in well-drained soil, thirteen pears
On limbs of scaled black bark and finest grain
Put forth white blossoms, toothed leaves, gritty fruit.

Last, over this rise that blocks my sight
Are set out fifty rows of various stock
Whose swelling grapes grow heavy through the year,
Each reaching its maturity in time,
The early purple yielding rich red wine,
The whites plucked late from dry Corinthian vines.

# DAVID MIDDLETON

I drank from every row to celebrate
The death of Priam and his fifty sons,
And yet from that old man's blood-encrusted face
So like my father's, I knew that even Zeus
Would find in a dead king's countenance his own
Gazing on Fate that brings all sons back home.

Yes, I am Odysseus! I alone survived
Poseidon, the Sirens, Circe, and the dead.
And yet to be the man beyond my fame
Required me to return to name these trees
That mark the place you, father, kept for me,
This middle world beside the Middle Sea.

## To a Scholar in the Stacks

When you began your story all its words
Had long been written down, its elements
Already so cohered in such exact
Equations that there should have seemed to be
No place to go, no entrance to the maze.
A heart less bold would have refused to start,
A mind less ignorant would have stayed home.

For Pasiphaë already had conceived
And borne her bully boy, and Daedalus
Responding had designed the darkness in
Its mystical divisions; Theseus,
Before you came, descended and returned,
By means of the thread, many and many a time.
What was there that had not been always done?

And still, when you began, only because
You did begin, the way opened before you.
The pictured walls made room, received your life;
Pasiphaë frowned, the Sea King greeted you,
And sighing Ariadne gave the thread
As always; in that celebrated scene
You were alone in being alone and new.

And now? You have gone down, you have gone in,
You have become incredibly rich and wise
From wandering underground. And yet you weary

And disbelieve, daring the Minotaur
Who answers in the echoes of your voice,
Holding the thread that has no other end,
Speaking her name whom you abandoned long ago.

Then out of this what revelation comes?
Sometimes in darkness and in deep despair
You will remember, Theseus, that you were
The Minotaur, the Labyrinth and the thread
Yourself; even you were that ingener
That fled the maze and flew — so long ago —
Over the sunlit sea to Sicily.

## *Summer's Elegy*

Day after day, day after still day,
The summer has begun to pass away.
Starlings at twilight fly clustered and call,
And branches bend, and leaves begin to fall.
The meadow and the orchard grass are mown,
And the meadowlark's house is cut down.

The little lantern bugs have doused their fires,
The swallows sit in rows along the wires.
Berry and grape appear among the flowers
Tangled against the wall in secret bowers,
And cricket now begins to hum the hours
Remaining to the passion's slow procession
Down from the high place and the golden session
Wherein the sun was sacrificed for us.
A failing light, no longer numinous,
Now frames the long and solemn afternoons
Where butterflies regret their closed cocoons.
We reach the place unripe, and made to know
As with a sudden knowledge that we go
Away forever, all hope of return
Cut off, hearing the crackle of the burn-
ing blade behind us, and the terminal sound
Of apples dropping on the dry ground.

## *For Robert Frost, in the Autumn in Vermont*

All on the mountains, as on tapestries
Reversed, their threads unreadable though clear,
The leaves turn in the volume of the year.
Your land becomes more brilliant as it dies.

The puzzled pilgrims come, car after car,
With cameras loaded for epiphanies;
For views of failure to take home and prize,
The dying tourists ride through realms of fire.

"To die is gain," a virgin's tombstone said;
That was New England, too, another age
That put a higher price on maidenhead
If brought in dead; now on your turning page
The lines blaze with a constant light, displayed
As in the maple's cold and fiery shade.

## HOWARD NEMEROV

# *World Lines*

*A War Story*

*And there I was*, is how these things begin,
Doing my final exam, a solo test
Of navigation by dead reckoning;
If you got there and back, you had to pass.

I got there in good shape, a mining town
Far north of nowheresville, and had turned for home
When the cloud closed down and the snow swept in,
Nothing but speeding snow and darkness white,

But I found the spur of a railroad headed south,
The Iron Compass, the Lost Flyer's Friend,
And followed that at a couple of hundred feet
Until it tunneled into the side of a hill,

And there I was. What then? What happened then?
Now who was I to know what happened then,
A kid just out of school the year before?
His buttons and bones are somewhere out there still.

Memorial Day, '86

## *O Crayola!*

*— for John Updike*

Shall we tell them thanks but why
reward us who, as children,
filled in time by filling in
coloring books? Or shall we lie?

O Crayola! — even the taste was good.

# JOYCE CAROL OATES

## *I Am Krishna, Destroyer of Worlds*

Another Monday morning!
At 30,000 feet hurtled through the "sky"!
What does it mean to dwell among strangers
with whom we would not wish to die?

# *Such Beauty!*

Through the night that thin sifting sound
and by morning the world's locked in ice:
a galaxy of ice-petal leaves,
all trees Ionic columns of light.

Such beauty looks permanent, doesn't it?

## Laocoön in Hades

*Ecce autem gemini a Tenedo tranquilla per alta —*
*Horresco referens — inmensis orbibus angues*
*Incumbunt pelago, pariterque ad litora tendunt,*
*Pectora quorum inter fluctus arrecta iubaeque*
*Sanguineae superant undas . . .*

— Aeneid *II, 203-207*

*From Tenedos, on the calm sea, twin snakes —*
*I shiver to recall it — endlessly*
*Coiling, uncoiling, swam abreast for shore,*
*Their underbellies showing as their crests*
*Reared red as blood above the swell . . .*

— *Fitzgerald, II, 280-284*

I saw them coming from the open sea —
Two red crests rode the waves, and four green eyes
Focused on me and mine, as if we were
The only prey available. I ran
Armed with a spear and naked sword — in vain.
They had already coiled round my boys
Choking them blue. I could not even stand
Up straight enough to make a proper cast
Or slash effectively. Two slimy loops
Fettered each ankle while a scaly grip
Held my back immobile. Then I felt
Those venomed teeth go rasping at my flesh:
Agony — but it had to be ignored.

# JOSEPH S. SALEMI

How could I save my children from a death
So vile and bestial that no Trojan dared
To look upon us as we suffered it?
No time to coddle pain — my single thought
Was to set free my limbs from that cold clasp
Of serpentine pollution. So I made
One final wrenching effort that released
My right arm for an instant, and I flailed
The swordblade wildly, uselessly, through air.
The snakes squeezed even tighter, and I watched
The last few fragments of my sons go down
Those hellish viper gullets. Father Zeus!
How could you sit in silence as this crime
Bloodied the earth? The boys were innocent.
I was the one who mocked the wooden horse;
I was the voice of warning to doomed Troy.
But your fell daughter took no note of that —
She killed two helpless children just to make
Their father out a liar. Now we sit
Here amidst all who perished in that place
By sword or sacrifice, disease or guile,
And none had a fouler, less becoming end
Than I, who died for speaking out the truth.
You smile, and muse about your several deaths:
Iphigeneia, dressed to be a bride,
But married to the sacrificial knife;
Achilles with an arrow in his heel
Shot by a mincing playboy, from behind;
Priam slaughtered like a common dog
At his own altar, while the family watched;
Poor Agamemnon, cut down in his bath

# JOSEPH S. SALEMI

By a deceitful, calculating wife;
Astyanax, flung from a precipice
To splatter on the hunching rocks below.
The Fates spun evil lots for most of you —
Nevertheless, allow me to insist
That those red-crested monsters were the cap
And summit of divine iniquity.
Never will I forgive, though eons pass,
The screaming of two sons, my futile rage,
And how Olympus looked on, unperturbed.

# *Penelope's Postscript*

Uncounted days, wrung dry of tears —
Lost wanderers do not return:
So much for the departed years.

Heap up my mangled hopes and fears,
Leave Ithaka to mock and spurn
Uncounted days. Wrung dry of tears

I shut from my importuned ears
The suitors' pleas. How could I yearn
So much for the departed? Years

Spent weaving shrouds amidst their jeers
(Feigned piety would serve my turn)
Uncounted days wrung dry. Of tears

I shed enough. My vision clears:
No longer am I keen to learn
So much for the departed years.

Out of the mist a man appears,
A revenant whose angers burn
Uncounted. Days, wrung dry of tears!
So much for the departed years.

# JOSEPH S. SALEMI

## Jove's Apologia To Juno For His Infidelity

*Quod licet Jovi, non licet bovi.*
*Rank has its privileges.*

My dear, of this you may be sure:
If I indulge a brief amour
With some young wench whom I have fancied
(Or shepherd boy fit to be nancied)
I have no wish to slight your state
Or let our nuptial vows abate.
Indeed, why should I foment strife
With you, my sister and my wife?
But gods, you know, have scant control —
In us, once kindled, passion's coal
Glows redder than old Vulcan's forge,
Impelling us to swill and gorge
As though our thirst and hunger raged
Like lions starved, and then uncaged.
I am great Jove, Immortal Sky —
Below me lands and oceans lie
All open to divine review.
Given such power, why eschew
The privileges of rank and pride?
Like the eagle, down I glide
To pluck what helpless prey I can.
In this, I differ from a man
Who, being mortal, rarely seizes

The bedmate that his fancy pleases.
*He* must cajole and ply and woo
With promises (and presents too!)
But when I see a young girl's hip
Curved like Diana's silver ship,
Or smell a dryad's unshorn hair
Heavy with scent of forest air,
Or lift a mermaid from the spume
That laps about her scaly womb,
Or hear a nubile wood-nymph squeal
In startled pleasure when I steal
Caresses from her velvet breast,
My blood grows hot . . . you know the rest.
Therefore, sweet consort, think not ill
Of your poor spouse, compelled to till
So many foreign fields. I trust
You see now that he simply *must*.

## *Pontius Pilate, A.D. 33*

> *What is Truth? said jesting Pilate, and would*
> *not stay for an answer.*
>
> — *Francis Bacon*

Where's Quintus? Has he brought the rescripts here?
I asked them of him seven hours past.
The merchants give us no peace with their cries
And Rome's dispatches have not yet been read.
Ill fortune that in busy times as these
I should be called to play a puppet judge
In the religious wranglings of the Jews.
Curse the zealots and their Holy Law!
Some prophet — Son of God, he calls himself —
Provoked the wrath of certain ancient priests,
And now the Hebrew rabble crowd the streets
Calling on Moses' law and Caesar's might
To send the hapless fellow to the cross.
He too, when offered freedom by Rome's law,
Stands in a trance, proclaims himself a king,
Heeds not the mob that clamors for his death,
Takes scourge and nails in witness of the Truth.

Truth! I have seen that Hydra oft before,
That twisting monster with the many heads.
Seize it here, it turns to seize you there;
Kill one head, it grows two more again.
The feverish offspring of some old Greek's brain —

# JOSEPH S. SALEMI

Where does it begin? Where does it end?
The bearded minions of philosophy,
Plato's fry and Aristotle's spawn,
Did they gain one more year upon this earth
In payment of their fruitless search for Truth?
Have they escaped the universal law
That more than Rome claims empire over men,
The awful, judging Fates who sentence all
To hang upon the final stake of death?
All are silent now — there are no words,
No tangled web-work to ensnare the minds
Of dreamy Greeks who talked much to no end.

Truth is a monster crueler than the cross —
He lures men on and makes wild beasts of them.
A Dionysos is this Truth indeed,
For drunken madmen are those seized by him.
See these Jews, a worthless desert race,
Thrashing about for ages in this land,
Conquered by Rome and brought under her sway,
Fit to be servile — obedient at the least —
To Rome, as Gaul and Cyrenaica are.
But no — because of Truth they will not serve,
Dream always of their kingdom for to come,
Trusting their God will overpower Rome,
Make Israel great and lordly over men,
And begin the reign of righteousness on earth.
This is their Truth — at least one part of it.
And yet here comes this Jesus to the fore,
Preaching of kingdoms, righteousness, and Truth;
He breaks some priestly law; he makes a sign

# JOSEPH S. SALEMI

That is forbidden on their Sabbath-day;
He says a word that goes against the grain
Of what some sunbaked prophet of their tribe
Wrote — who knows when? — in their crumbling scrolls.
Off to the cross he goes — because of Truth.

I spoke to him before they took him off:
A pious rabbi — but Dionysos-led!
He had within his eyes the burning fire
That always flashes upward or away.
His speech a glimpse of hidden meaning showed
That marks the speaker as not of this world.
Did I not move to save his wretched life,
To rein the vengeance of his frenzied tribe,
To let him live, and flee far from this land?
No — he will have none of it, the fool,
But walks off as a man within a dream
Who skirts the edge of pitfalls heedlessly.

Well, let them wrangle — Rome will get along
With or without them, and without their Truth.
There is only Fate, and man, and Time,
And of those three, the first and last have sway
Over poor man, and bend him to their will.
The Truth, like phantom water on the sand,
Beckons the parched to drink what is not there,
Then vanishes away, while calling forth
New dreams and visions to beguile new men.
Rome will not chase the lure of fantasy,
Pursuing kingdoms in the upper air.
Let Truth go even like this prophet Christ
Wide-eyed to Golgotha to start his reign.

# WILLIAM JAY SMITH

## *Rear Vision*

The cars in the mirror come swiftly forward,
While I, in thought, move slowly back;
Time past (reflected) seems to wind
Along the boundaries of mind,
A highway cold, distinct, and black.
Who knows to what the years have led,
And at which turning up ahead —
On the white-stitched road reflected back —
The furies gather in a pack,
While all the sky above burns black,
Unwinding still the darkening thread?

# WILLIAM JAY SMITH

## *Death of a Jazz Musician*

I dreamed that when I died a jukebox played,
And in the metal slots bright coins were laid;
Coins on both my eyes lay cold and bright
As the boatman ferried my thin shade into the night.

I dreamed a jukebox played. I saw the flame
Leap from a whirling disc which bore my name,
Felt fire like music sweep the icy ground —
And forward still the boatman moved, and made no sound.

# WILLIAM JAY SMITH

## *A Green Place*

I know a place all fennel-green and fine
Far from the white ice cap, the glacial flaw,
Where shy mud hen and dainty porcupine
Dance in delight by a quivering pawpaw;

Dance by catalpa tree and flowering peach
With speckled guinea fowl and small raccoon,
While the heron, from his perforated beach,
Extends one bony leg beyond the moon.

I know a place so green and fennel-fine
Its boundary is air; and will you come?
A bellflower tinkles by a trumpet vine,
A shrouded cricket taps a midget drum.

There blue flies buzz among the wild sweet peas;
The water speaks: black insects pluck the stream.
May apples cluster there by bearded trees,
Full-skirted dancers risen from a dream.

Birds call; twigs crackle; wild marsh grasses sway;
Will you come soon, before the cold winds blow
To swirl the dust and drive the leaves away,
And thin-ribbed earth pokes out against the snow?

# WILLIAM JAY SMITH

## *Words by the Water*

*From* Three Songs

Beneath the dimming gardens of the sky
That ship, my heart, now rides its anchor chain;
A room is harbor when the world's awry
And life's direction anything but plain.
Still is the wind, and softer still the rain.
*Sleep in my arms, my love. O sleep, my love.*

Time hangs suspended: with its floating farms,
Its peacock-green and terraced atmosphere,
Now sleep awaits us, love. Lie in my arms;
It is not death but distance that I fear,
Dark is the day, and dangerous the year.
*Sleep in my arms, my love. O sleep, my love.*

# W. D. SNODGRASS

## *April Inventory*

The green catalpa tree has turned
All white; the cherry blooms once more.
In one whole year I haven't learned
A blessed thing they pay you for.
The blossoms snow down in my hair;
The trees and I will soon be bare.

The trees have more than I to spare.
The sleek, expensive girls I teach,
Younger and pinker every year,
Bloom gradually out of reach.
The pear tree lets its petals drop
Like dandruff on a tabletop.

The girls have grown so young by now
I have to nudge myself to stare.
This year they smile and mind me how
My teeth are falling with my hair.
In thirty years I may not get
Younger, shrewder, or out of debt.

The tenth time, just a year ago,
I made myself a little list
Of all the things I'd ought to know,
Then told my parents, analyst,
And everyone who's trusted me
I'd be substantial, presently.

# W. D. SNODGRASS

I haven't read one book about
A book or memorized one plot.
Or found a mind I did not doubt.
I learned one date. And then forgot.
And one by one the solid scholars
Get the degrees, the jobs, the dollars.

And smile above their starchy collars.
I taught my classes Whitehead's notions;
One lovely girl, a song of Mahler's.
Lacking a source-book or promotions,
I showed one child the colors of
A luna moth and how to love.

I taught myself to name my name,
To bark back, loosen love and crying;
To ease my woman so she came,
To ease an old man who was dying.
I have not learned how often I
Can win, can love, but choose to die.

I have not learned there is a lie
Love shall be blonder, slimmer, younger;
That my equivocating eye
Loves only by my body's hunger;
That I have forces, true to feel,
Or that the lovely world is real.

While scholars speak authority
And wear their ulcers on their sleeves,
My eyes in spectacles shall see

## W. D. SNODGRASS

These trees procure and spend their leaves.
There is a value underneath
The gold and silver in my teeth.

Though trees turn bare and girls turn wives,
We shall afford our costly seasons;
There is a gentleness survives
That will outspeak and has its reasons.
There is a loveliness exists,
Preserves us, not for specialists.

# W. D. SNODGRASS

## *The Survivors*

We wondered what might change
Once you were not here;
Tried to guess how they would rearrange
Their life, now you were dead. Oh, it was strange
Coming back this year —

To find the lawn unkept
And the rock gardens dense
With bindweed; the tangling rosebushes crept
And squandered over everything except
The trash by the fence;

The rose trellises blown
Down and still sprawled there;
Broken odd ends of porch furniture thrown
Around the yard; everything overgrown
Or down in disrepair.

On the tree they still protect
From the ungoverned gang
Of neighbor boys — eaten with worms, bird-pecked,
But otherwise uncared-for and unpicked,
The bitter cherries hang,

Brown and soft and botched.
The ground is thick with flies.
Around in front, two white stone lions are crouched

# W. D. SNODGRASS

By the front steps; someone has patched
Cement across their eyes.

The Venetian blinds are drawn;
Inside, it is dark and still.
Always upon some errand, one by one,
They go from room to room, vaguely, in the wan
Half-light, deprived of will.

Mostly they hunt for some-
thing they've misplaced; otherwise
They turn the pages of magazines and hum
Tunelessly. At any time they come
To pass, they drop their eyes.

Only at night they meet.
By voiceless summoning
They come to the living room; each repeats
Some words he has memorized; each takes his seat
In the hushed, expectant ring

By the television set.
No one can draw his eyes
From that unnatural, cold light. They wait.
The screen goes dim and they hunch closer yet,
As the image dies.

In the cellar where the sewers
Rise, unseen, the pale white
Ants grow in decaying stacks of old newspapers.

# W. D. SNODGRASS

Outside, street lamps appear, and friends of yours
Call children in for the night.

And you have been dead one year.
Nothing is different here.

## *Looking*

What was I looking for today?
All that poking under the rugs,
Peering under the lamps and chairs,
Or going from room to room that way,
Forever up and down the stairs
Like someone stupid with sleep or drugs.

Everywhere I was, was wrong.
I started turning the drawers out, then
I was staring in at the icebox door
Wondering if I'd been there long
Wondering what I was looking for.
Later on, I think I went back again.

Where did the rest of the time go?
Was I down cellar? I can't recall
Finding the light switch, or the last
Place I've had it, or how I'd know
I didn't look at it and go past.
Or whether it's what I want, at all.

# W. D. SNODGRASS

## *The Last Time*

Three years ago, one last time, you forgot
Yourself and let your hand, all gentleness,
Move to my hair, then slip down to caress
My cheek, my neck. My breath failed me; I thought

It might all come back yet, believed you might
Turn back. You turned, then, once more to your own
Talk with that tall young man in whom you'd shown,
In front of all our friends, such clear delight

All afternoon. You recalled, then, the long
Love you had held for me was changed. You threw
Both arms around him, kissed him, and then you
Said you were ready and we went along.

# Hades Welcomes His Bride

Come now, child, adjust your eyes, for sight
Is here a lesser sense. Here you must learn
Directions through your fingertips and feet
And map them in your mind. I think some shapes
Will gradually appear. The pale things twisting
Overhead are mostly roots, although some worms
Arrive here clinging to their dead. Turn here.
Ah. And in this hall will sit our thrones,
And here you shall be queen, my dear, the queen
Of all men ever to be born. No smile?
Well, some solemnity befits a queen.
These thrones I have commissioned to be made
Are unlike any you imagined; they glow
Of deep-black diamonds and lead, subtler
And in better taste than gold, as will suit
Your timid beauty and pale throat. Come now,
Down these winding stairs, the air more still
And dry and easier to breathe. Here is a room
For your diversions. Here I've set a loom
And silk unraveled from the finest shrouds
And dyed the richest, rarest shades of black.
Such pictures you shall weave! Such tapestries!
For you I chose those three thin shadows there,
And they shall be your friends and loyal maids,
And do not fear from them such gossiping
As servants usually are wont. They have
Not mouth nor eyes and cannot thus speak ill

Of you. Come, come. This is the greatest room;
I had it specially made after great thought
So you would feel at home. I had the ceiling
Painted to recall some evening sky —
But without the garish stars and lurid moon.
What? That stark shape crouching in the corner?
Sweet, that is to be our bed. Our bed.
Ah! Your hand is trembling! I fear
There is, as yet, too much pulse in it.

# A. E. STALLINGS

## *Eurydice Reveals Her Strength*

Dying is the easy part.
As you still live, my dear, why did you come?
You should learn an easing of the heart
As I have, now, for truly some

Prefer this clarity of mind, this death
Of all the body's imperious demands:
That constant interruption of the breath,
That fever-greed of eyes and hands

To digest your beauty whole.
You strike a tune upon a string:
They say that it is beautiful.
You sing to me, you sing, you sing.

I think, how do the living hear?
But I remember now, that it was just
A quiver in the membrane of the ear,
And love, a complicated lust.

And I remember now, as in a book,
How you pushed me down upon the grass and stones,
Crushed me with your kisses and your hands and took
What there is to give of emptiness, and moans.

We strained to be one strange new beast enmeshed,
And this is what we strained against, this death,

And clawed as if to peel away the flesh,
Crawled safe inside another's hollowness,

Because we feared this calm of being dead.
I say this. You abhor my logic, and you shiver,
Thinking I may as well be just some severed head
Floating down a cool, forgetful river,

Slipping down the shadows, green and black,
Singing to myself, not looking back.

# A. E. STALLINGS

## Crazy to Hear the Tale Again (The Fall of Troy)

> *". . . ferit aurea sidera clamor"*
> — *Virgil,* Aeneid *2.488*

The stars were golden! Golden as the fire —
We had seen nothing like it, ah, but then
Such things that night, we'll not see such again.
But stars, we'd thought, were purer, somehow: higher —

And yet it seemed a blush that turned them gold.
What once was chill alike to joy or harm
That one strange night seemed somehow to grow warm
And dashed the hopes long cherished by the Old

That Nature was a white and mindless thing
Of perfect mathematical design
As snowflakes are, as blameless and as fine
(For lo, the stars grew gold and maddening).

Yes, there were horrors hinted in that night.
I thought a veil was parted from my eyes
And thought I saw our gods, of monstrous size,
Splash barefoot in our blood, and with delight.

# A. E. STALLINGS

## *The Wife of the Man of Many Wiles*

Believe what you want to. Believe that I wove,
If you wish, twenty years, and waited, while you
Were knee-deep in blood, hip-deep in goddesses.

I've not much to show for twenty years' weaving —
I have but one half-finished cloth at the loom.
Perhaps it's the lengthy, meticulous grieving.

Explain how you want to. Believe I unravelled
At night what I stitched in the slow siesta,
How I kept them all waiting for me to finish,

The suitors, you call them. Believe what you want to.
Believe that they waited for me to finish,
Believe I beguiled them with nightly un-doings.

Believe what you want to. That they never touched me.
Believe your own stories, as you would have me do,
How you only survived by the wise infidelities.

Believe that each day you wrote me a letter
That never arrived. Kill all the damn suitors
If you think it will make you feel better.

# A. E. STALLINGS

## *Menielle*

I've dragged my weary feet home after dusk
And a day of boiling tea and burning milk.
Long have I toiled at the thankless task.

I've done the washing up, smiled through my mask,
Taken dictation and jobs of that ilk
And dragged my weary feet home after dusk.

Some give orders who could simply ask
In voices hissing soft as rustled silk.
Long have I toiled at the thankless task

And long have I made change, and made it brisk,
Though nothing changes: customers carp and bilk,
& I drag my weary feet home after dusk.

To soothe the angry, I have tapped the cask
Of patience dry, and nursed them through their sulk.
Long have I toiled at the thankless task

And wished I could glare like a basilisk
Or Medusa, but I'm the one who turns to chalk,
Dragging my stony feet home after dusk.
Long have I toiled at the thankless task.

## *Practice*

The basketball you walk around the court
Produces a hard, stinging, clean report.
You pause and crouch and, after feinting, swoop
Around a ghost defender to the hoop
And rise and lay the ball in off the board.
Solitude, plainly, is its own reward.

The game that you've conceived engrosses you.
The ball rolls off; you chase it down, renew
The dribble to the level of your waist.
Insuring that a sneaker's tightly laced,
You kneel — then, up again, weave easily
Through obstacles that you alone can see.

And so I drop the hands I'd just now cupped
To call you home. Why should I interrupt?
Can I be sure that dinner's ready yet?
A jumpshot settles, snapping, through the net;
The backboard's stanchion keeps the ball in play,
Returning it to you on the ricochet.

## TIMOTHY STEELE

# Beatitudes, While Setting Out the Trash

The sparrow in the fig tree cocks his head
And tilts at, so to speak, his daily bread
(The sunset's stunningly suffused with gold).
A squirrel on the lawn rears and inspects
A berry in its paws and seems to hold
The pose of a Tyrannosaurus Rex.

The clothesline's plaids and stripes perform some snaps;
A page of blown newspaper smartly wraps
A fire hydrant in the day's events;
And there's engaging, if pedestrian, song
Ringing its changes from a chain-link fence
A boy with a backpack walks a stick along.

I park my rattling dolly at the curb
And set the trash among leaves gusts disturb.
Then, hands tucked in my sweatshirt's pocket-muff,
A mammal cousin of the kangaroo,
I watch my breath contrive a lucent puff
Out of lung-exhalated $CO_2$.

Small breath, small warmth, but what is that to me?
My steps re-traced, the bird's still in his tree:
He grooms, by nuzzling, a raised underwing;
He shakes and sends a shiver through his breast,
As if, from where he perches, counseling
That *Blessed are the meek*, for they are blest.

## TIMOTHY STEELE

## *Portrait of the Artist as a Young Child*

Your favorite crayon is Midnight Blue
(Hurrah for dark dramatic skies!)
Though inwardly it makes you groan
To see it like an ice-cream cone
Shrink with too zealous exercise.

But soon you're offering for review
Sheets where Magenta flowers blaze.
And here's a field whose mass and weight
Incontrovertibly indicate
You're in your Burnt Sienna phase.

Long may you study color, pore
Over Maroon, Peach, Pine Green, Teal.
I think of my astonishment
When I first saw the spectrum bent
Around into a color wheel,

A disc of white there at the core,
The outer colors vivid, wild.
Red, with its long wavelengths, met
With much-refracted violet,
And all with all were reconciled.

When I look past you now, I see
The winter amaryllis bloom

Above its terra-cotta pot
Whose earthen orange-apricot
Lends warmth to the entire room.

And cherry and mahogany
Introduce tones of brown and plum;
While by the hearth a basket holds
Balls of yarn — purples, greens, and golds
That you may wear in years to come.

Yet for the moment you dispense
Color yourself. Again you kneel:
Your left hand spread out, holding still
The paper you'll with fervor fill,
You're off and traveling through the wheel

Of contrasts and of complements,
Where every shade divides and blends,
Where you find those that you prefer,
Where being is not linear,
But bright and deep, and never ends.

## *Advice to a Student*

Frame your excuse, when your work is late,
    By Aristotelian laws.
It is essential that your fate
    Derive from a credible cause.
Fill the instructor with pity and fear:
    You mustn't be afraid
To fabricate deaths of the near and dear
    If this will serve your grade.

Gods-from-machines won't help you pass.
    Only the inept say,
*As I was bringing my essay to class,*
    *Boreas blew it away.*
Don't get too tricky; unify;
    Keep your tale under control;
Make each part of the alibi
    Suit the organic whole.

Always present yourself as one
    Who, neither saint nor god,
Didn't quite get the assignment done,
    Being tragically flawed.
Art judges not only deeds, but intentions;
    Much is allowed to youth.
You may win pardon by means of inventions
    That supercede the truth.

# TIMOTHY STEELE

## *Joseph*

The fridge clicks, hums; light flows across
Cold sleeping tiles, and I survey
Red chilies, lime juice, tartar sauce —
Things I can't use or throw away
And which, some hours from morning, wear
An aspect of profound despair.

A glass of milk? Perhaps some food?
I draw a carton from the back.
Ranged on the wall by magnitude,
Knives gleam on their magnetic rack.
Novitiate-like, I stand before
The cylinder of white I pour.

What woke me? Was it that I sensed
The far drone of a passing plane?
I drink, then lean my head against
The chill damp of the windowpane,
And all the while the ticking clock's
Like a plain, baffling paradox.

Each quick, clenched moment's like the next.
Yet time yields shape and history.
I think — disquieted, perplexed —
How Joseph knelt at Pharaoh's knee
As he leaned from his throne to hear
The meaning of his dreams made clear

And luminous, for once, with hope.
When I look up I see in space
The moon as through a telescope:
Vague winds cross, streamingly, its face,
Remote and icy and antique,
And to its light I whisper, Speak.

# *The Dance at St. Gabriel's*

*for Louis Otto*

We were the smart kids of the neighborhood
where, after high school, no one went to school,
you NYU and I CCNY.
We eyed each other at St. Gabriel's
on Friday nights, and eyed each other's girls.
You were the cute, proverbial good catch
— just think of it, nineteen — and so was I,
but all we had was moonlight on our minds.
This made us cagey; we would meet outside
to figure how to dump our dates, go cruising.
In those hag-ridden and race-conscious times
we wanted to be known as anti-fascists,
and thus get over our Italian names.
When the war came, you volunteered, while I
backed in by not applying for deferment,
for which my loving family named me Fool.
Once, furloughs overlapping, we met up,
the Flight Lieutenant and the PFC;
we joked about the pair we made, and sauntered.
That Father Murray took one look at us,
and said our Air Force wings were the only wings
we'd ever earn. We lofted up our beers.
Ah, Louis, what good times we two have missed.
Your first time up and out the Germans had you,
and for your golden wings they blew you down.

# FELIX STEFANILE

## *Soldiers and Their Girls*

*(First Three-Day Pass)*

Those years before Fast Food a pizza meant
a neighborhood, an accent maybe, or
the way the customers looked. You had your limits.
One train-stop more it might be Fish and Chips,

or Blintzes. What a way to spend a date,
skipping from joint to joint, and getting drunk
on laughter and strange sipping, stupid jokes
about the squid, rose-water, or flat-bread.

Whatever, down it went. You smiled and smiled
because the girl was pretty and proud
and scared. She wanted you to know
Armenians were just like you, or Jews,

and we were all Americans anyway.
You checked your watch, said "Hitler!" She teared up,
pert Rosie Ohanessian, whose large eyes
were darker than that last night on your mind.

She walked you to the depot. You held hands,
but never made a move, the station crammed,
young couples slouching, grinning, waiting for
the speaker to announce the bus from camp.

## FELIX STEFANILE

---

# *On Painting a Bike*

The weather, like a tourist here before,
returns in patch and plaid to lawn and tree;
three robins repossess the courteous shore
of our brick lake, and scold the continent.
The children's bicycles are blue this year;
I wonder now what last year's colors meant.

In my own childhood, when the weather came,
April or May, I felt a busy need
to be at painting — it was like a game
of changing all the furniture of the earth,
made up of bikes and wagons it would seem;
I brushed away for all that I was worth.

I took such satisfaction in my stain
I caused the garden in the back to glow,
and those old irons glimmered in the rain
like famous weapons fabulous to win.
Mine was a landscape painted over then
might make a proper serpent change his skin.

Now I'm turning gray; the season's green;
there's not a single fault that I can dye.
Some kids ride past, each eager to be seen,
with arms outspread, like wings, as after all
I did myself once, till I had a spill
that skinned me red as Eden in the fall.

# *Taking Sides with John Ciardi*

*— some words on minus-American poetry*

When Robert Lowell hyphenated you —
Italian, hyphen sign, American —
to praise your poetry, your answer ran
in rough-house expletives. Your passion flew,
and subsequently in an interview
you squelched his harmless seeming little hyphen
as not the way to write out citizen.
How culture-vultures smiled at the to-do.

If this is poetry, as may be true,
it's also punctuation, not too thin
a point or line for morals that you drew.
We all know grammar can stick like a pin,
and those who think my point is overdrawn,
they are no friends of yours, nor of mine, John.

## *Breakings*

Long before I first left home, my father
tried to teach me horses, land, and sky,
to show me how his kind of work was done.
I studied how to be my father's son,
but all I learned was, when the wicked die,
they ride combines through barley forever.

Every summer I hated my father
as I drove hot horses through dusty grass;
and so I broke with him, and left the farm
for other work, where unfamiliar weather
broke on my head an unexpected storm
and things I had not studied came to pass.

So nothing changes, nothing stays the same,
and I have returned from a broken home
alone, to ask for a job breaking horses.
I watch a colt on a long line making
tracks in dust, and think of the kinds of breakings
there are, and the kinds of restraining forces.

# *Goodbye to the Old Friends*

Because of a promise I cannot break
I have returned to my father's house, and here,
for the first time in years, I have risen
early this Sunday to visit the Friends.
As I drive to the Meeting House, the trees
wave softly as the wind moves over me.

I am late. Faces turn to look at me;
I sit in a pew apart, and silence breaks
slightly, like the rustle of old trees.
I wonder whether I am welcome here,
but in the old wall clock I see a friend.
An old man I remember now has risen

to say that this is Easter. Christ has risen.
The ticking of the old wall clock distracts me
as this old man addresses his friends;
he prowls for an hour through a Bible, breaks
his voice to bring my wandering mind back here
from aimless circling through the aging trees

whose branches tick like clocks. Boughs cut from trees,
disposed through the room, remind me of the risen
Christ this voice speaks of; I do not see him here.
I do not see him here, but flowers tell me,
on the mantel before us, in scent that breaks
above the graying heads of nodding Friends,

on hats and in lapels of aging Friends,
the flowers and the branches from the trees
remind me of what this old man's voice breaks
for the last time to tell us:  Christ has risen.
With the tongue of a man he speaks to me
and to his Friends:  there are no angels here.

At last I shout without breath my first prayer here
and ask for nothing but silence. Two old Friends
turn slowly toward each other, letting me
know how much silence remains. The trees
ripple the silence, and the spirit has risen.
Two old hands of marble meet and Meeting breaks.

Old Friends move over the lawn, among old trees.
One offers me his hand. I have risen,
I am thinking, as I break away from here.

# HENRY TAYLOR

## *An Afternoon of Pocket Billiards*

Here where there is neither hope nor haste
all my days blend; each dark day is misplaced
    inside my crowded head.
I try to beat a game, half chance, half cold
and steady practice, struggling for the skill
that might kill chance. But chance's claws take hold,
the game is wrecked, and time is all I kill:
no sleight of hand or heart can overcome
the fear that, in this darkness, only time
    is not already dead.

I narrow down my gaze to where I waste
days growing used to a dusty taste
    that hangs in the dead air;
motes of chalk and talcum powder sift
down past the hard edge of the swinging light
above my table. Jukebox voices drift
by me through the dark, raveled with a slight
vibration from that older world beyond
the window:  now I listen for a sound
    that may still rise somewhere

    this afternoon, away
from here . . . my eyes wander from where I play
to the motions of more skillful hands than mine:
another player leans above his cue.
Between us, those old tremors seem to move

# HENRY TAYLOR

the air I stare through, almost as if you
were breathing here:  that half-remembered love
    obscures the perfect shot
I turned to watch; I turn back, but am caught
between my past and the shifting design

on a green field of order where I wait
for time and strength of will to dissipate
    these shapes that coil and turn
above the hush and click of herded spheres.
Brief glimpses of a chain of treacheries
flicker around a melody that bears
into this room the gradual disease
we fled when you tore blindly out our driveway
for the last time, and I came here to play,
    to wait for your return,

for this game's random shifts to bring you back
or set me free. As I blunder through each rack,
    no two shots are the same;
yet if, beneath them all, dim certainties
evolve to hold my called shots on a course
that weaves beyond love's sudden vagaries,
still, an impulse like love, in the force
behind that wavering song, caroms my thought
into an old mistake:  with every shot
    I call, I speak your name.

High and low, striped and solid balls rotate
in endless formations as time grows late.
    My concentration breaks

just at the dead-reckoned instant before
each shot: testing stroke and angle, I ease
down on the felt and line it up once more;
too late, I feel that slight vibration seize
my arm — too late to stand. My knocking heart
shatters skill and chance, and takes the game apart.
  I make my own mistakes.

I chalk my cue and call for one more rack,
believing I might still untwist the wreck
  your song makes in my head.
I think how spellbound Bottom woke to shout
through nightmare trees, "When my cue comes, call me,
and I will answer . . ." Your voice might find me out,
note by note unraveling to recall me
from this enchanted wood beyond your reach.
"When my cue comes . . ." Moving only by touch,
  I try to hold the thread,

listening for the words to an old song
that draws me down, sets me adrift among
  patterns below the game.
The words will not connect. Red blood and bone,
older than love, the swirling echo drives
me down below green felt toward solid stone
whose grains read out the sequence of my lives
in sounds like underwater footsteps. My blind
and whispering fingers stroke the stone to find
  strength to forget the shame

I learned too long ago. I may be wrong
to follow an ancient, dimly-sounding song
    whose melody is fear,
whose words might never speak; but now I know
that in it, somewhere, forces of hand and will
combine like dancers on a stage. And now,
within the strictness of my touch, I feel
a surge of steadiness. I rise to air,
to dust and vacant noise and old despair.
    Error still holds me here,

    but I'll be right someday:
though one song of old love has died away,
an older song is falling into place.
From now on I will play to make it speak,
to see the form its words give to this game.
I see, as I move into another rack,
that all days in this cavern are the same:
    endless struggles to know
how cold skill and a force like love can flow
together in my veins, and be at peace.

Here where there is neither hope nor haste
I narrow down my gaze to where I waste
    this afternoon away;
on a green field of order, where I wait
for this game's random shifts to bring you back,
high and low, striped and solid balls rotate.
I chalk my cue and call for one more rack,
listening for the words to an old song
I learned too long ago: "I may be wrong,
    but I'll be right someday."

# San Francesco d'Assisi: Canticle of Created Things

Thine be the praise, good Lord
omnipotent, most high, Thine
the honor, the glory, and every blessing.
To Thee alone, most high, do these belong;
to speak Thy name no living man is worthy.

Be praised, my Lord, with all that Thou hast made;
above all else the sun, our master and our brother,
whence Thy gift of daylight comes.
He is most fair, and radiant with great splendor,
and from Thee, most high, his meaning comes.

Be praised, my Lord, for our sister moon,
        and for the stars;
Thou hast placed in the heavens their clear
        and precious beauty.
Be praised, my Lord, for our brother wind
and for the air, in all weathers cloudy and clear,
whence comes sustenance for all which Thou hast made.

Be praised, my Lord, for our sister water,
who is most useful, precious, humble and pure.

Be praised, my Lord, for our brother fire,
for Thine is the power by which he lights the dark;
Thine are his beauty and joy, his vigor and strength.

Be praised, my Lord, for earth, our mother
and our sister;
by Thy power she sustains and governs us,
and puts forth fruit in great variety, with grass
and colorful flowers.

Be praised, my Lord, for those who forgive
by the power of Thy love within them,
for those who bear infirmities and trials;
blessed are those who endure in peace,
for Thou at last shalt crown them, O most high.

Be praised, my Lord, for our sister bodily death,
from whom no living man escapes;
woe unto those who die in mortal sin,
but blessed be those whom death shall find
living by thy most sacred wishes,
for through the second death no harm
shall come to them.

Praise my Lord and give thanks unto Him;
bless my Lord and humbly serve Him.

# FREDERICK TURNER

## *From* Two Poems

If I could touch you with my secret heart
Or warm your fingers with my dearest breath
I would, my love; your coldness is like death
And senseless tissue seals up every part.

If your lips' snow should ever turn to dew
Or your turn ever come again to speak
It could not be my doing. I am weak
Each muscle neither knows nor does what it should do.

In this cold country summer never comes.
In my hands even secrets never keep.
They die, and all their brightness goes to sleep.
Your softness hardens and your touching numbs.

I kill when most I mean to cherish; you
Are my cold queen, despite all I can do.

---

# *At the Casa Paredes*

*Santiago de Compostela*

It always rains my last night in a city:
It did in Skopje, Wellington, and Seoul.
The windows mist, I order something hearty,
The cold wet cobbles shimmer in my soul.

And now I drink white wine in Santiago,
As car-tires hiss outside, and plates are stacked;
Black windows flash the waitress's imago,
And all life seems to be a play, an act.

I'm just a pilgrim in this rainy weather,
And now each thing I do, I do again;
Everything's passing into dark together,
And still I celebrate the thin fine rain.

Taking, as always, a poet's time with dying,
It looks as if I'm going to close this place;
This stupid heart, so much in love with being,
Would play the soul, for just an evening's grace.

# FREDERICK TURNER

## *After the Conference*

I'm stuck, alone, at night, in Germany.
The hotel room is comfortable and bare.
I see now all my naïve vanity.
It's raining outside in the lamplit square.
I'm nearly fifty-nine, and still my folly
Keeps me awake with sweating and remorse;
I toss in an exhausted melancholy
And each new memory just makes it worse.
I strut through life, a sentimental fraud,
Refusing to admit when things go wrong,
Believe them when they courteously applaud,
Try to stand out, pretend that I belong.
God, now I lie before you, old and tired,
Twelve hours more travel, and I cannot sleep;
Why should you listen now, since I ignored
Your mercies when success ran full and deep?
An early car goes past. I leave at five.
How strange how sweet it is to be alive.

# FREDERICK TURNER

## *The Kite*

As if a little girl had come to you
Asking for help to fly her birthday kite,
And you stretched out the silk, set the struts true,
So the device was feathery, strung, and tight;

And on a hillside blown with the spring light,
It lifted from her hands into the blue,
And tugged so fiercely that you gave it flight
And up it went, wind-drawn (as if you knew
The whole skill of the kitemasters that flew
Those painted Chinese kites designed to fight
Before an emperor and his retinue);

Such is the book that I would want to write,
Whose power could haul a mile of line into
The dark purple, and strangely out of sight.

# JOHN UPDIKE

## *Dry Spell*

In Arizona's drought, even cacti
die; the prickly pears are pancake-flat
with no more rain to plump them up, and blanch
to lavender instead of green. Iraq
continues like a curtainless bad play,
the Tucson *Star* headlines the daily bust,
and Barry Bonds limps close to Babe Ruth's record.
Amid all this, I age another notch.

Dear Lord, have I become too poor a thing
to save? My pencil creeps across this page
unsure where next to go. My children phone
from far-off islands, all their lives in flux
while mine has petrified, a desert rock
to take their superstitious bearings by.

\*

Today my mate of thirty years and I
explored the grid that fills our foothills view
and bought two oleander plants to screen
our porch from passing cars, or them from us.
How touchingly we scrambled on the rocks,
our footing poor, to pour out MiracleGro
(the blue of Listerine) on wilting plants
that mutely guard our island in the sun.

## JOHN UPDIKE

She gave me, at my own discreet request,
a dictionary of words I keep
forgetting, and a watch whose battery
is guaranteed to last ten years, at least.
Ten years! It will tick in my coffin while
my bones continue to deteriorate.

\*

Our view — in other seasons, of the North
Atlantic, luminous and level, fringed
by greenery that goes, all imperceptibly,
from bud to leaf to blaze to cold bare twig —
at night resembles, in its lateral sweep,
the other one, two thousand miles away.
The city, in its valley lying flat
as golden water, twinkles, ripples, breathes,

streetlights deflected downward to avoid
bleaching the sky for the observatories
whose giant geared and many-mirrored eyes
peer upward from some local mountaintops.
These mountains hang to the south like blue clouds
that would, back east, past Hull and Hingham, bring rain.

# JOHN UPDIKE

## *Thoughts While Driving Home*

Was I clever enough? Was I charming?
  Did I make at least one good pun?
Was I disconcerting? Disarming?
  Was I wise? Was I wan? Was I fun?

Did I answer that girl with white shoulders
  Correctly, or should I have said
(Engagingly), "Kierkegaard smolders,
  But Eliot's ashes are dead"?

And did I, while being a smarty,
  Yet some wry reserve slyly keep,
So they murmured, when I'd left the party,
  "He's deep. He's deep. He's deep"?

# *Authors' Residences*

*After Visiting Hartford*

Mark Twain's opinion was, he was entitled
  To live in style; his domicile entailed
Some seven servants, nineteen rooms, unbridled
    Fantasies by Tiffany
    That furnished hospitality
With tons of stuff, until the funding failed.

The poet Wallace Stevens, less flamboyant,
  Resided in a whiter Hartford home,
As solid as his neighbors', slated, *voyant*
    For all its screening shrubs; from here
    He strolled to work, his life's plain beer
Topped up with Fancy's iridescent foam.

And I, I live (as if you care) in chambers
  That number two — in one I sleep, alone
Most nights, and in the other drudge; my labors
    Have brought me to a little space
    In Boston. Writers, know your place
Before it gets too modest to be known.

# JOHN UPDIKE

## *The Sometime Sportsman Greets the Spring*

When winter's glaze is lifted from the greens,
And cups are freshly cut, and birdies sing,
Triumphantly the stifled golfer preens
In cleats and slacks once more, and checks his swing.

This year, he vows, his head will steady be,
His weight-shift smooth, his grip and stance ideal;
And so they are, until upon the tee
Befall the old contortions of the real.

So, too, the tennis-player, torpid from
Hibernal months of television sports,
Perfects his serve and feels his knees become
Sheer muscle in their unaccustomed shorts.

Right arm relaxed, the left controls the toss,
Which shall be high, so that the racket face
Shall at a certain angle sweep across
The floated sphere with gutty strings — an ace!

The mind's eye sees it all until upon
The courts of life the faulty way we played
In other summers rolls back with the sun.
Hope springs eternally, but spring hopes fade.

# RICHARD WAKEFIELD

## *The Bell Rope*

In Sunday school the boy who learned a psalm
by heart would get to sound the steeple bell
and send its tolling through the Sabbath calm
to call the saved and not-so-saved as well.
For lack of practice all the lines are lost
— something about how angels' hands would bear
me up to God — but on one Pentecost
they won me passage up the steeple stair.
I leapt and grabbed the rope up high to ride
it down, I touched the floor, the rope went slack,
the bell was silent. Then, beatified,
I rose, uplifted as the rope pulled back.
I leapt and fell again; again it took
me up, but still the bell withheld its word —
until at last the church foundation shook
in bass approval, felt as much as heard,
and after I let go the bell tolled long
and loud as if repaying me for each
unanswered pull with heaven-rending song
a year of Sunday school could never teach
and that these forty years can not obscure.
Some nights when sleep won't come I think of how
just once there came an answer, clear and sure.
If I could find that rope I'd grasp it now.

# RICHARD WAKEFIELD

## *Learning by a Narrow Light*

It's thirty years yet I recall
at unexpected moments all
our hours in that room we shared
those afternoons, how sunlight glared
outside but only reached a thin
illuminating line within,
between the windowsill and blind,
across the floor, the bed, to find
in all that darkness two so graced
as we were, lying there embraced.
In moments when we lay at rest
(there were a few) I saw your breast,
your face, some random part of you
that line of sunlight fell onto.
The narrow band of sunlight showed
me tiny golden hairs that glowed
against your skin, a freckle here
and there, all precious, perfect, clear
and isolate because that light,
so narrow, narrowed down my sight.
By limiting how much I saw
it showed me more, as if to draw
you as I watched, and when the sun
had moved its strip of light and done
its slow and gracious glide I'd learned
what I could never have discerned
in naked light. My greedy eye

# RICHARD WAKEFIELD

was slowed and taught to satisfy
itself with less that's really more,
the less that isn't too much for
a man to see and really see.
And now that light comes back to me
and nothing can recall so much
as it my vision, like a touch,
caressing you, and I so young
and close to losing you among
the overwhelming all of you.
It seems as if that sunlight knew
the danger there. And so it goes
today, each sunlit moment shows
me more, another precious part
to add to all I've learned by heart.

# *The Searcher*

I found him sitting back against a tree
as autumn's evening sun fell slant and dim.
The old man looked no more confused to me
than those who'd sent me there to look for him.
They found his pickup at the trailhead
and knew he'd wandered off along the trail.
They'd take his keys, his wife and daughter said,
and put him someplace for the old and frail.
And now I'd be a hero. I walked across
the rusty duff, raising dust to climb
through streaks of light and treading layered moss
of countless winters, but slow, to give him time,
though time was what I knew I couldn't give.
His eyes were dim with age and dusk, but clear
enough to ask me not to make him live,
to say no wandering had brought him here.
I had a half a mind to walk away,
to let him be, with darkness falling fast,
and he had more than half a mind to stay.
And then I radioed for help at last.
I sat myself beside him, breathed the blended
scents of sweat and dust and pitchy bark,
until our wordless span of waiting ended
as flashlights flickered toward us in the dark.

# DEREK WALCOTT

## *Fight with the Crew*

*From* The Schooner *Flight*

It had one bitch on board, like he had me mark —
that was the cook, some Vincentian arse
with a skin like a gommier tree, red peeling bark,
and wash-out blue eyes; he wouldn't give me a ease,
like he feel he was white. Had an exercise book,
this same one here, that I was using to write
my poetry, so one day this man snatch it
from my hand, and start throwing it left and right
to the rest of the crew, bawling out, "Catch it,"
and start mincing me like I was some hen
because of the poems. Some case is for fist,
some case is for tholing pin, some is for knife —
this one was for knife. Well, I beg him first,
but he keep reading, "O my children, my wife,"
and playing he crying, to make the crew laugh;
it move like a flying fish, the silver knife
that catch him right in the plump of his calf,
and he faint so slowly, and he turn more white
than he thought he was. I suppose among men
you need that sort of thing. It ain't right
but that's how it is. There wasn't much pain,
just plenty blood, and Vincie and me best friend,
but none of them go fuck with my poetry again.

# DEREK WALCOTT

## *A Latin Primer*

*In Memoriam: H. D. Boxill*

I had nothing against which
to notch the growth of my work
but the horizon, no language
but the shallows in my long walk

home, so I shook all the help
my young right hand could use
from the sand-crusted kelp
of distant literatures.

The frigate bird my phoenix,
I was high on iodine,
one drop from the sun's murex
stained the foam's fabric wine;

ploughing white fields of surf
with a boy's shins, I kept
staggering as the shelf
of sand under me slipped,

then found my deepest wish
in the swaying words of the sea,
and the skeletal fish
of that boy is ribbed in me;

but I saw how the bronze
dusk of imperial palms
curled their fronds into questions
over Latin exams.

I hated signs of scansion.
Those strokes across the line
drizzled on the horizon
and darkened discipline.

They were like Mathematics
that made delight Design,
arranging the thrown sticks
of stars to sine and cosine.

Raging, I'd skip a pebble
across the sea's page; it still
scanned its own syllable:
trochee, anapest, dactyl.

*Miles*, foot soldier. *Fossa*,
a trench or a grave. My hand
hefts a last sand bomb to toss
at slowly fading sand.

I failed Matriculation
in Maths; passed it; after that,
I taught Love's basic Latin:
*Amo, amas, amat.*

# DEREK WALCOTT

In tweed jacket and tie
a master at my college
I watched the old words dry
like seaweed on the page.

I'd muse from the roofed harbour
back to my desk, the boys'
heads plunged in paper
softly as porpoises.

The discipline I preached
made me a hypocrite;
their lithe black bodies, beached,
would die in dialect;

I spun the globe's meridian,
showed its sealed hemispheres,
but where were those brows heading
when neither world was theirs?

Silence clogged my ears
with cotton, a cloud's noise;
I climbed white tiered arenas
trying to find my voice,

and I remember: it was on a
Saturday near noon, at Vigie,
that my heart, rounding the corner
of Half-Moon Battery,

# DEREK WALCOTT

stopped to watch the foundry
of midday cast in bronze
the trunk of a gommier tree
on a sea without seasons,

while ochre Rat Island
was nibbling the sea's lace,
that a frigate bird came sailing
through a tree's net, to raise

its emblem in the cirrus,
named with the common sense
of fishermen: sea scissors,
*Fregata magnificens*,

*ciseau-la-mer*, the patois
for its cloud-cutting course;
and that native metaphor
made by the strokes of oars,

with one wing beat for scansion,
that slowly levelling V
made one with my horizon
as it sailed steadily

beyond the sheep-nibbled columns
of fallen marble trees,
or the roofless pillars once
sacred to Hercules.

# DEREK WALCOTT

## *Menelaus*

Wood smoke smudges the sea.
A bonfire lowers its gaze.
Soon the sand is circled with ugly
ash. Well, there were days

when, through her smoke-grey
eyes, I saw the white trash that was
Helen: too worn-out to argue
with her Romany ways.

That gypsy constancy,
wiry and hot, is gone;
firm hill and wavering sea
resettle in the sun.

I would not wish her curse
on any: that necks should spurt,
limbs hacked to driftwood, because
a wave hoists its frilled skirt.

I wade clear, chuckling shallows
without armour now, or cause,
and bend, letting the hollows
of cupped palms salt my scars.

Ten years. Wasted in quarrel
for sea-grey eyes. A whore's.

## DEREK WALCOTT

Under me, crusted in coral,
towers pass, and a small sea-horse.

# DEREK WALCOTT

## *A Far Cry from Africa*

A wind is ruffling the tawny pelt
Of Africa. Kikuyu, quick as flies,
Batten upon the bloodstreams of the veldt.
Corpses are scattered through a paradise.
Only the worm, colonel of carrion, cries:
"Waste no compassion on these separate dead!"
Statistics justify and scholars seize
The salients of colonial policy.
What is that to the white child hacked in bed?
To savages, expendable as Jews?

Threshed out by beaters, the long rushes break
In a white dust of ibises whose cries
Have wheeled since civilization's dawn
From the parched river or beast-teeming plain.
The violence of beast on beast is read
As natural law, but upright man
Seeks his divinity by inflicting pain.
Delirious as these worried beasts, his wars
Dance to the tightened carcass of a drum,
While he calls courage still that native dread
Of the white peace contracted by the dead.

Again brutish necessity wipes its hands
Upon the napkin of a dirty cause, again
A waste of our compassion, as with Spain,
The gorilla wrestles with the superman.

# DEREK WALCOTT

I who am poisoned with the blood of both,
Where shall I turn, divided to the vein?
I who have cursed
The drunken officer of British rule, how choose
Between this Africa and the English tongue I love?
Betray them both, or give back what they give?
How can I face such slaughter and be cool?
How can I turn from Africa and live?

# DEBORAH WARREN

## *Lullaby in Blue*

Maybe I could paint you the way to sleep
more easily than singing you there with notes.
Before beginning, though, I'd want the blue,
older than time, that waited over the deep
before the daylight shook the earth awake;
I'd cover the brash night with as many coats
of darkness as the thin blue air would take.

Composing sleep, I'd imitate the jewels
strung through the night to give the night dimension;
I'd draft the space to let you travel through
the stars until you're with them, in suspension,
sampling infinity for an hour or two
before the morning. But I'll only break
the palette and brush and stir you with loud red love.

## DEBORAH WARREN

# *Marginalia*

Finding an old book on a basement shelf —
gray, spine bent — and reading it again,
I met my former, unfamiliar, self,
some of her notes and scrawls so alien
that, though I tried, I couldn't get (behind
this gloss or that) back to the time she wrote
to guess what experiences she had in mind,
the living context of some scribbled note;

or see the girl beneath the purple ink
who chose this phrase or that to underline,
the mood, the boy, that lay behind her thinking —
but they were thoughts I recognized as mine;

and though there were words I couldn't even read,
blobs and cross-outs; and though not a jot
remained of her old existence — I agreed
with the young annotator's every thought:

A clever girl. So what would she see fit
to comment on — and what would she have to say
about the years that she and I have written
since — before we put the book away?

# *El Greco's* Burial of Count Orgaz

*Church of Santo Tomé, Toledo*

If that parish asked *me* to portray
two saints attending Count Orgaz's grave?
"I'll paint your miracle, Santo Tomé,"
I'd say, "but you're commissioning *my* view.
A soul ascending to the sky?" I'd say,
"It's not one picture at all; it's really two.
You can't fit earth and heaven on one canvas
cozily." So, yes, this is the way

I'd lay it out:  The body down below,
heavy in armor, lifted to the tomb;
the noble mourners in a sober row,
black-clad behind the two attendant saints.
Useless for Stephen and Augustine to glow
(dressed as they are in bright celestial paints —
jeweled mitre, gold-brocaded copes):
The somber foreground makes a dull tableau.

Above, though! Lord-a-mercy! — wind and whirl!
It's laundry day in heaven, and the clouds
are hanging out to dry. And through their curl
and stream an angel makes a thoroughfare,
piercing them with a chrysalis of pearl:
This is the dead knight's soul. A hank of air,

it's of one substance with the vaporous clouds
whose silver sheets the Judge's hands unfurl.

Stiffly dividing earth from sky, and even
stiffer in their sad gravity, the nobles
wear their beards like spades. Do they believe in
miracles? The descent of Augustine?
What are these men who watch this painted Stephen?
Sinners? Saints? They're something in between,
El Greco says. Not animal — not angel.
What do these men have to do with heaven?

The oil-soul in aqueous ascension?
Show me in a burette. Let me observe
the particles in a man with some pretension —
at his burial — to a plane divine.
El Greco's picture paints us a suspension
of the disbelief that draws the line
at saints come from the clouds in starry gold:
You bright saints! Are you more than bright invention?

Thomas, be our patron. In a stole
like Augustine's, attend us. Make us more
than protons, more than mourners daubed in oil,
jaws half-haloed in the Vs of ruffs.
Make us the priest whose filmy surplice rolls
back from his wrist and shows his cassock cuffs
black as decay — who spreads his arms with grace
enough to clothe his body with a soul.

## DEBORAH WARREN

# *Prospect and Retrospect*

*Epithalamion for C. and J.*

Imagine years from today, when a mirror
(blurred opaque with the vapor from a bath)
clings to a film of steam and the damp June morning
as if it wants to absorb the silver air
into its skin; and when you lift your fingers,
clearing the surface is no easy thing:

As soon as you wipe the glass, steam-saturated
droplets re-collect in heavy beads —
in heavier silver runnels you erase
again, with your whole arm, wrist to elbow, finding —
losing — finding — a handsome woman's face.

Rub again, and the drying glass goes clearer —
backward into the years, from layer down to the layer
underneath, and the woman gets less gray —
and earlier, parting the veils of vapor, back
through happiness and happiness, and back
to the heart-shaped face of the girl you are today:

There — it's the present; and from the mirror
now, with the mist rubbed off, floats out a song:
The song, with the scent of apples and of flowers,
echoes the tune of light you walk along
reflecting and following you — to then from now.

**GAIL WHITE**

## *Queen Gertrude's Soliloquy*

I wish he wouldn't sulk. It's unbecoming,
and first impressions ought to be our best.
Then I do wish he'd stop that beastly humming
and talking to himself. "Give it a rest —
you're acting out!"  I long to say, but no,
a mother can't, that's being interfering.
Of course he was at school, and ought to go
again, but Claudius gets hard of hearing
if I bring that up. As for other means —
Ophelia? She's a darling, but not quite
The sort of character one wants in queens —
all sugar and no spice. She'd never fight
his weaknesses. But there's another chance:
I'll send for Guildenstern and Rosencrantz . . .

## *Simone de Beauvoir to Sartre*

I never make unpleasant scenes.
We're free of bourgeois bonds. Which means
That you, my love, are wholly free
To relish infidelity.

I do not cry when every spring
You have your adolescent fling
With some enchanting ingénue
For am not I as free as you?

And I shall tell biographers
We had two freedoms — his and hers.
And freedom made our love endure,
We were so damnably mature.

**GAIL WHITE**

---

## *For a Senior Killed on Prom Night*

It's useless to pretend you would have been
a genius. I taught you and I know.
You made the team, but others made it win.
A ready smile made up for being slow.

You'd have been ordinary in the end:
the hardest worker someone ever had,
one woman's husband and one man's best friend,
recipient of cards for "world's best dad."

So why, where you'd have been, is there a blank
so huge, a hole where all thoughts go to die?
The world has only lost one of its rank
and file. You didn't even make me cry.

Why do I go outside at one a.m.
and search the stars as though I'd numbered them?

# RICHARD WILBUR

## *The Ride*

The horse beneath me seemed
To know what course to steer
Through the horror of snow I dreamed,
And so I had no fear,

Nor was I chilled to death
By the wind's white shudders, thanks
To the veils of his patient breath
And the mist of sweat from his flanks.

It seemed that all night through,
Within my hand no rein
And nothing in my view
But the pillar of his mane,

I rode with magic ease
At a quick, unstumbling trot
Through shattering vacancies
On into what was not,

Till the weave of the storm grew thin,
With a threading of cedar-smoke,
And the ice-blind pane of an inn
Shimmered, and I awoke.

How shall I now get back
To the inn-yard where he stands,

Burdened with every lack,
And waken the stable-hands

To give him, before I think
That there was no horse at all,
Some hay, some water to drink,
A blanket and a stall?

# RICHARD WILBUR

## *The Writer*

In her room at the prow of the house
Where light breaks, and the windows are tossed with linden,
My daughter is writing a story.

I pause in the stairwell, hearing
From her shut door a commotion of typewriter-keys
Like a chain hauled over a gunwale.

Young as she is, the stuff
Of her life is a great cargo, and some of it heavy:
I wish her a lucky passage.

But now it is she who pauses,
As if to reject my thought and its easy figure.
A stillness greatens, in which

The whole house seems to be thinking,
And then she is at it again with a bunched clamor
Of strokes, and again is silent.

I remember the dazed starling
Which was trapped in that very room, two years ago;
How we stole in, lifted a sash

And retreated, not to affright it;
And how for a helpless hour, through the crack of the door,
We watched the sleek, wild, dark

# RICHARD WILBUR

And iridescent creature
Batter against the brilliance, drop like a glove
To the hard floor, or the desk-top,

And wait then, humped and bloody,
For the wits to try it again; and how our spirits
Rose when, suddenly sure,

It lifted off from a chair-back,
Beating a smooth course for the right window
And clearing the sill of the world.

It is always a matter, my darling,
Of life or death, as I had forgotten. I wish
What I wished you before, but harder.

## *Peter*

There at the story's close
We could not stay awake.
The new wine made us doze,
And not for Jesus' sake

I struck the high-priest's slave
Who came at start of day,
But as a hand might wave
Some bugling fly away.

That hand warm by the flame,
I murmured no, no, no
To mutters of his name
And felt the rooster's crow

Flail me, yet did not waken
Out of that rocky sleep.
Dungeoned I stood there, shaken
Only enough to weep,

Only enough to fill,
At those predicted jeers,
Through the dropped lashes' grille
The socket's moat of tears.

# RICHARD WILBUR

## *Cottage Street, 1953*

Framed in her phoenix fire-screen, Edna Ward
Bends to the tray of Canton, pouring tea
For frightened Mrs. Plath; then, turning toward
The pale, slumped daughter, and my wife, and me,

Asks if we would prefer it weak or strong.
Will we have milk or lemon, she enquires?
The visit seems already strained and long.
Each in his turn, we tell her our desires.

It is my office to exemplify
The published poet in his happiness,
Thus cheering Sylvia, who has wished to die;
But half-ashamed, and impotent to bless,

I am a stupid life-guard who has found,
Swept to his shallows by the tide, a girl
Who, far from shore, has been immensely drowned,
And stares through water now with eyes of pearl.

How large is her refusal; and how slight
The genteel chat whereby we recommend
Life, of a summer afternoon, despite
The brewing dusk which hints that it may end.

And Edna Ward shall die in fifteen years,
After her eight-and-eighty summers of

Such grace and courage as permit no tears,
The thin hand reaching out, the last word *love*,

Outliving Sylvia who, condemned to live,
Shall study for a decade, as she must,
To state at last her brilliant negative
In poems free and helpless and unjust.

## GREG WILLIAMSON

---

## *Italics, Mine*

*Hello, up there. Thank God you happened by.*
          *I'm touched. I've been beneath the covers*
     *For so long now the light is stark,*
*Where honestly I thought that I might lie*
     *Alone forever in the dark,*
          *And this is a place for lovers.*

*By night I dreamed about the day you looked*
          *And read my thoughts and would agree*
     *To spend some time with me, and talk.*
*Since all the flights to Paris have been booked,*
     *Perhaps you'd settle for a walk*
          *To see what we shall see.*

*You see that oak leaf there? I always sense*
          *A kinship with the leaves. To me*
     *Each one portrays a little oak,*
*A fragile replica of an immense*
     *Black oak, itself a lush, baroque,*
          *Green forest of a tree.*

*And at the shore let's walk the water line,*
          *The ocean's flexing, outermost*
     *Advance, where the seawater laps*
*A sandy beach, plotting a jagged line*
     *Whose every subdivision maps*
          *A continental coast.*

*Or looking backward toward the mountain range,*
*We see the ridge line's collarbone,*
*Comprising summit and ravine,*
*And holding up a rock we find a strange,*
*Profound affinity between*
*The mountains and the stone.*

*If I seem to be beginning to repeat*
*Myself, it is because the world*
*Repeats itself in hidden laws*
*Whose figurings and fractals the exegete*
*Tries to articulate because*
*In the beginning was the word.*

*As with the sense of humor in a laugh,*
*In every word a poem survives,*
*Abundantly rich in ways and means*
*To build the sentence and the paragraph,*
*The rise and fall of little scenes,*
*The stories of our lives.*

*The coming home of walks and talks and stories*
*Discloses what we came to know,*
*Where the changing fortunes of a day*
*Become a lifetime's sadnesses and glories,*
*A stranger's face to which we say,*
*As to the mirror, "Hello."*

*Hello. I hope you pardon my conceits,*
*But I have dreamed on my nightstands*
*From all these little rooms to build*

# GREG WILLIAMSON

*A home where we might lie between the sheets,*
  *And I declare myself fulfilled*
    *When I am in your hands.*

*But this has all been talk, I know, and I*
        *Can tell you are about to turn*
  *And go your way, while I repair*
*To darkness and a dateless night. Goodbye.*
  *I will be saying a silent prayer*
      *That one day you return.*

# *From* On the International Date Line

II.
Midway in the Pacific, our acolyte
Lights out across the Date Line heading west,
Where time unravels and the days rewrite,

As though upon a scrolling palimpsest,
Recycled daily like *The Daily Globe*,
The subplots of our interweaving geste

With a cast of billions and a vast wardrobe.
If we could straddle that imagined fence
Between the dates of our diurnal strobe,

If briefly we could leave the present tense,
Where all our flawed performances are live,
And read the past's account of our expense,

Recast a scene, rewrite the narrative,
If we could read the stage directions for
Some future act, to find where we arrive. . . .

But no. And you have heard this all before.
We cannot see what sights we will have seen,
And all we ever saw is nevermore.

# GREG WILLIAMSON

III.
The International Date Line lies between
Two continents, in the middle of the sea.
As with the dark stage following a scene

Or the white space which divides an elegy,
One cannot say just when the days exhume
Themselves, deep in that darkness, quietly.

But when the lights go up and words resume,
The new world seems, itself, a world apart
And written in a novel nom de plume,

Except this tragic drama is not art,
With its rehearsals and its rubber swords.
Each actor gets one reading of his part

And opening night, alone, to tread the boards.
We pay in time for the little time we borrow,
And lull ourselves to sleep by looking towards

Tomorrow and tomorrow and tomorrow,
The bedside words of all our yesterdays,
A sorry promise promising more sorrow.

## GREG WILLIAMSON

# *The Man in the Window*

At night in lighted rooms, who has not seen
His dark reflection in the glass,
    His countenance impose
    On the cold rains and snows
That fall in the world beyond the glass,
As if his figure figured in that scene?

On the bus I used to ride
To school, I watched my image fly
Across the fixed addresses as they flew
Across the window I was looking through,
    Where he was passed or passing by
    The permanent outside.

Looking out, I have seen him looking in
    At the schoolboy suddenly alone,
    The man across the mall
    Or far end of the hall,
The boyfriend on the telephone,
The stranger playing poker where I'd been.

    Somehow I cannot say
Just how the haunting haunted eyes
Have seemed to dream disparate worlds together:
I am projecting him on rainy weather,
    But looking back in my disguise
    He's watching what I say.

# GREG WILLIAMSON

Oh I know it's fanciness — the interface
  · Shows just the figure I expect,
       No ghost, no shadowy Cain,
       But rather me again
  Learning the ins and outs — except
All night the dog's been snarling at that face.

# GREG WILLIAMSON

## *Up in the Air*

Gin-weary, temple on the pane,
I watch the props begin to shake
The sunlight. As we climb, the plane
Trolls its crank bait shadow across a lake.

It drags an airy grappling hook
Over the churches of white towns
Tucked away in the hills that look,
For all their pleated folds, like dressing gowns

Where all the clouds are shaving cream
And powder, periwigs and lace,
The fragments of a lazy dream
That conjures up a ballroom in their place

And finds, across the dreamt parquet,
In a cirrus gown, a girl. Then all
At once this cloying matinee
Dissolves, as if the episodes I call

My life were just such master strokes
Of whimsy, false and protean,
And all I think I love a hoax
Invented by the shadow of a man

Muttering in a windowseat,
Watching a toothless anchor comb

A lake, fooled by his own conceit.
At most, from all of this, someone at home

May shake his head in a reading chair
Or glance up from a gin and lime
At this annoyance in the air,
A minor thing which happens all the time.

# Acknowledgments

DICK ALLEN. "On the New Haven Line," "*William Rimmer*: Flight and Pursuit," "The Swing," and "Backstroking at Thrushwood Lake" are from *Ode to the Cold War: Poems New and Selected*. Copyright © 1997 by Dick Allen. Reprinted with the permission of Sarabande Books, www.sarabandebooks. org.

WILLIAM BAER. "The '2' Train" and "Andrew" are published with the permission of the author. "Eclipse" is from *"Borges" & Other Sonnets*, Truman State University Press. Copyright © 2003. Reprinted with the permission of the author. "The Shipmaster's Note" is from *The Unfortunates*, New Odyssey Press. Copyright © 1997. Reprinted with the permission of the author.

JIM BARNES. "The Sawdust War," "Under the Tent," and "On Hearing the News That Hitler Was Dead" are from *The Sawdust War*, University of Illinois Press. Copyright © 1992. Reprinted with the permission of the author. "Bathing in Lethe" and "MIA" (from "Bombardier") are from *La Plata Cantata* (from *On a Wing of the Sun: Three Volumes of Poetry*), University of Illinois Press. Copyright © 2001. Reprinted with the permission of the author.

RAY BRADBURY. "To Ireland . . . ," "Go Not with Ruins in Your Mind," and "Byzantium I Come Not From" are from *I Live By The Invisible: New & Selected Poems*, Salmon Publishing, Ltd. Copyright © 2002. Reprinted with the permission of the author.

GWENDOLYN BROOKS. "the preacher: ruminates behind the sermon" (from "A Street in Bronzeville"), "gay chaps at the bar," "piano after war," "mentors" (from "Gay Chaps at the Bar"), "The Children of the Poor" (from "The Womanhood"), and "We Real Cool" are from *Selected Poems*, Harper & Row. Copyright © 1963. Reprinted by consent of Brooks Permissions.

CATHARINE SAVAGE BROSMAN. "Burning in Louvain" is from the 112.1 (Winter 2004) issue of *The Sewanee Review*. Reprinted with the permission of the author.

ROBERT DASELER. "At the Barrier," "14 Tamalpais Street," "Night Fog," and "Shadows" are from *Levering Avenue*, University of Evansville Press. Copyright © 1998. Reprinted with the permission of the author.

JAMES DICKEY. "Reading *Genesis* to a Blind Child," "On the Hill Below

266

SAMUEL MAIO. "From the Notebooks of Count Galeazzo Ciano," "Love Song," "Pilate," "Projections," and "The Paintings of Arnesti Gaspári" are from *The Burning of Los Angeles*, Thomas Jefferson University Press. Copyright © 1997. Reprinted with the permission of the author.

CHARLES MARTIN. "Lot's Wife Looks Back" and "Neither Here nor There" (from "A Walk in the Hills above the Artists' Home") are from *Starting from Sleep: New and Selected Poems*. Copyright © 2002. Reprinted with the permission of Overlook Press.

DAVID MASON. "The Pond" and "Letter to No Address" are from *The Country I Remember*, Story Line Press. Copyright © 1996. Reprinted with the permission of the author. "*Agnostos Topos*" is from *Arrivals*, Story Line Press. Copyright © 2004. Reprinted with the permission of the author.

JOSHUA MEHIGAN. "A Cellar in Pankow," "In the Home of My Sitter," "Schism by Twilight," "Alexandra," and "Merrily" are from *The Optimist*, Ohio University Press. Copyright © 2004. Reprinted with the permission of Ohio University Press, www.ohioswallow.com, and with the permission of the author.

ROBERT MEZEY. "A Coffee House Lecture," "A Note She Might Have Left," "No Country You Remember," "Back," and "After Ten Years" are from *Collected Poems, 1952-1999*, University of Arkansas Press. Copyright © 2000. Reprinted with the permission of the author.

DAVID MIDDLETON. "The Sunday School Lesson" and "A Quiet Reply" are from *Beyond the Chandeleurs*. Copyright © 1999. Reprinted with the permission of Louisiana State University Press. "The Craft of Noah" (from "The Middle World") and "The Naming of the Trees: Odysseus to Laertes" are from *The Burning Fields*. Copyright © 1991. Reprinted with the permission of Louisiana State University Press.

HOWARD NEMEROV. "To a Scholar in the Stacks," "Summer's Elegy," "For Robert Frost, in the Autumn in Vermont," and "World Lines" are from *Trying Conclusions: New and Selected Poems 1961-1991*, University of Chicago Press. Copyright © 1991. Reprinted with the permission of Margaret Nemerov.

JOYCE CAROL OATES. "O Crayola!," "I Am Krishna, Destroyer of Worlds," and "Such Beauty!" are from *Tenderness*, The Ontario Review Press. Copyright © 1996. Reprinted with the permission of the author.

JOSEPH S. SALEMI. "Laocoön in Hades" and "Penelope's Postscript" are from *Formal Complaints*, Somers Rocks Press. Copyright © 1997. Reprinted with the permission of the author. "Jove's Apologia to Juno for His Infidelity" is from *Masquerade*, Pivot Press. Copyright © 2005. Reprinted with the permission of the author. "Pontius Pilate, A. D. 33" is published with the permission of the author.

WILLIAM JAY SMITH. "Rear Vision," "Death of a Jazz Musician," "A

# Contributors

DICK ALLEN lives in Trumbull, Connecticut. His books include *Present Vanishing: Poems* (2008), *The Day Before: New Poems* (2003), and *Ode to the Cold War: Poems New and Selected* (1997), all published by Sarabande Books.

WILLIAM BAER lives in Evansville, Indiana. His books include *"Bocage" and Other Sonnets* (Texas Review Press, 2008), *The Ballad Rode into Town* (Turning Point Books, 2007), and *Luís de Camões: Selected Sonnets* (University of Chicago Press, 2005).

JIM BARNES lives in Santa Fe, New Mexico. His books include *Visiting Picasso* (2007), *On a Wing of the Sun: Three Volumes of Poetry* (2001), and *Paris* (1997), all published by the University of Illinois Press.

RAY BRADBURY lives in Los Angeles, California. His books of poetry include *I Live By The Invisible: New & Selected Poems* (Salmon Publishing, Ltd., 2002) and *The Complete Poems of Ray Bradbury* (Ballantine Books, 1982), and his fiction includes *Fahrenheit 451* (Ballantine Books, 1953), and *The Martian Chronicles* (Doubleday, 1950).

GWENDOLYN BROOKS (1917-2000) received the Pulitzer Prize for *Annie Allen* (Harper & Brothers, 1949). Her other books include *Blacks* (David Company, 1987), *Aloneness* (Broadside Press, 1971), and *Selected Poems* (Harper & Row, 1963).

CATHARINE SAVAGE BROSMAN lives in Houston, Texas.

Her books include *Range of Light* (2007), *The Muscled Truce* (2003), both published by Louisiana State University Press, and *Finding Higher Ground: A Life of Travels* (University of Nevada Press, 2003).

ROBERT DASELER lives in Sacramento, California. He is the author of *Levering Avenue* (University of Evansville Press, 1998), and his work has been published in *London Magazine, The Formalist,* and *The Chicago Review.*

JAMES DICKEY (1923-1997) is the author of *The Whole Motion: Collected Poems, 1945-1992* (Wesleyan University Press, 1992), the novel *Deliverance* (Houghton Mifflin, 1970), and *Babel to Byzantium: Poets & Poetry Now* (Farrar, Straus and Giroux, 1968).

RHINA P. ESPAILLAT lives in Newburyport, Massachusetts. Her books include *El olor de la Memoria: Cuentos / The Scent of Memory: Short Stories* (Ediciones CEDIBIL, Santo Domingo, República Dominicana, 2007), *Playing at Stillness* (Truman State University Press, 2005), and *The Shadow I Dress In* (David Robert Books, 2004).

JONATHAN GALASSI lives in New York City. His books include *North Street* (HarperCollins, 2000), *Eugenio Montale: Collected Poems, 1920-1954* (Farrar, Straus and Giroux, 1998), and *Morning Run* (Paris Review Editions, 1988).

R. S. GWYNN lives in Beaumont, Texas. His books include *No Word of Farewell: Selected Poems 1970-2000* (Story Line Press, 2001), *The Drive-In* (University of Missouri Press, 1986), and *The Narcissiad* (Cedar Rock Press, 1981).

RACHEL HADAS lives in New York City. Her books include *The River of Forgetfulness* (David Robert Books, 2006), *Laws*

(Zoo Press, 2004), and *Halfway Down the Hall: New and Selected Poems* (Wesleyan University Press, 1998).

ANTHONY HECHT (1923-2004) received the Pulitzer Prize for *The Hard Hours* (Atheneum, 1967). His other books include *Collected Later Poems* (Alfred A. Knopf, 2003), *Melodies Unheard: Essays on the Mysteries of Poetry* (Johns Hopkins University Press, 2003), and *Collected Earlier Poems* (Alfred A. Knopf, 1990).

A. M. JUSTER lives in Belmont, Massachusetts. His books include *The Satires of Horace* (University of Pennsylvania Press, 2008), *The Secret Language of Women* (University of Evansville Press, 2002), and *Longing for Laura: A Selection of New Petrarch Translations* (Birch Brook Press, 2001).

X. J. KENNEDY lives in Lexington, Massachusetts. His books include *In a Prominent Bar in Secaucus: New and Selected Poems* (Johns Hopkins University Press, 2007), *Peeping Tom's Cabin: Comic Verse 1928-2008* (BOA Editions, 2007), and *Nude Descending a Staircase* (Doubleday, 1961).

LEN KRISAK lives in Newton, Massachusetts. His books include *The Odes of Horace* (Carcanet, 2006), *If Anything* (WordTech Editions, 2004), and *Even As We Speak* (University of Evansville Press, 2000).

ANTHONY LOMBARDY lives in Nashville, Tennessee. His books include *Antique Collecting* (WordTech Editions, 2004) and *Severe* (Bennett & Kitchel, 1995; Revised Edition, WordTech Editions, 2004).

SAMUEL MAIO lives in Northern California. His books include *The Burning of Los Angeles* (Thomas Jefferson University Press, 1997) and *Creating Another Self: Voice in Modern American*

*Personal Poetry* (Truman State University Press, 2005).

CHARLES MARTIN lives in Syracuse, New York. His books include *Metamorphoses*, by Ovid (W.W. Norton, 2004), *Starting from Sleep: New and Selected Poems* (Overlook Press, 2002), and *What the Darkness Proposes: Poems* (Johns Hopkins University Press, 1996).

DAVID MASON lives in Colorado Springs, Colorado. His books include *Ludlow* (Red Hen Press, 2007), *Arrivals* (Story Line Press, 2004), and *The Country I Remember* (Story Line Press, 1996).

JOSHUA MEHIGAN lives in Brooklyn, New York. He is the author of *The Optimist* (Ohio University Press, 2004), and his work has been published in *The New York Times*, *Poetry*, and *Ploughshares*.

ROBERT MEZEY lives in Pomona, California. His books include *Collected Poems, 1952-1999* (University of Arkansas Press, 2000), *Thomas Hardy: Selected Poems*, editor (Penguin Books, 1998), and *Evening Wind* (Wesleyan University Press, 1987).

DAVID MIDDLETON lives in Thibodaux, Louisiana. His books include *The Habitual Peacefulness of Gruchy: Poems After Pictures by Jean-François Millet* (2005), *Beyond the Chandeleurs* (1999), and *The Burning Fields* (1991), all published by Louisiana State University Press.

HOWARD NEMEROV (1920-1991) received the Pulitzer Prize for *The Collected Poems of Howard Nemerov* (University of Chicago Press, 1977). His other books include *Trying Conclusions: New and Selected Poems 1961-1991* (University of Chicago Press, 1991) and *Figures of Thought: Speculations on the Meaning of Poetry* (David R. Godine, 1978).

JOYCE CAROL OATES lives in Princeton, New Jersey. Her books of poetry include *Tenderness* (The Ontario Review Press, 1996), *Invisible Woman: New & Selected Poems 1970-1982* (The Ontario Review Press, 1982), and *The Fabulous Beasts* (Louisiana State University Press, 1975).

JOSEPH S. SALEMI lives in New York City. His books include *The Lilacs on Good Friday* (New Formalist Press, 2007), *Masquerade* (Pivot Press, 2005), and *Formal Complaints* (Somers Rocks Press, 1997).

WILLIAM JAY SMITH lives in Cummington, Massachusetts. His books include *Words by the Water* (Johns Hopkins University Press, 2008), *The Cherokee Lottery* (Curbstone Press, 2000), and *The World Below the Window: Poems 1937-1997* (Johns Hopkins University Press, 1998).

W. D. SNODGRASS lives in Erieville, New York. He received the Pulitzer Prize for *Heart's Needle* (Alfred A. Knopf, 1959). His other books include *Not for Specialists: New and Selected Poems* (BOA Editions, Ltd., 2006), *Make-Believes: Verses and Visions* (Eatonbrook Editions, 2004), and *De/Compositions: 101 Good Poems Gone Wrong* (Graywolf Press, 2001).

A. E. STALLINGS lives in Athens, Greece. Her books include *The Nature of Things*, by Lucretius (Penguin, 2007), *Hapax* (Northwestern University Press, 2006), and *Archaic Smile* (University of Evansville Press, 1999).

TIMOTHY STEELE lives in Los Angeles, California. His books include *Toward the Winter Solstice* (Swallow Press/Ohio University Press, 2006), *The Color Wheel* (Johns Hopkins University Press, 1994), and *Sapphics Against Anger and Other*

*Poems* (Random House, 1986).

FELIX STEFANILE lives in West Lafayette, Indiana. His books include *The Country of Absence: Poems and an Essay* (Bordighera Press, 2000), *The Dance at St. Gabriel's: Poems* (Story Line Press, 1995), and *If I Were Fire: Thirty-four Sonnets of Cecco Angiolieri* (Windhover Press, 1987).

HENRY TAYLOR lives in Pierce County, Washington. He received the Pulitzer Prize for *The Flying Change* (Louisiana State University Press, 1985). His other books include *Crooked Run* (2006), *Brief Candles: 101 Clerihews* (2000), and *Understanding Fiction: Poems 1986-1996* (1996), all published by Louisiana State University Press.

FREDERICK TURNER lives in Richardson, Texas. His books include *Paradise: Selected Poems, 1990-2003* (David Robert Books, 2004), *On the Field of Life, On the Battlefield of Truth* (Pivot Press, 2004), and *Genesis: An Epic Poem* (Saybrook Publishing Company, 1988).

JOHN UPDIKE lives in Beverly Farms, Massachusetts. He twice has received the Pulitzer Prize for fiction, the first for *Rabbit Is Rich* (Alfred A. Knopf, 1981) and the second for *Rabbit At Rest* (Alfred A. Knopf, 1990). His books of poetry include *Americana and Other Poems* (Alfred A. Knopf, 2001), *Collected Poems 1953-1993* (Alfred A. Knopf, 1993), and *The Carpentered Hen and Other Tame Creatures: Poems* (Harper & Brothers, 1958).

RICHARD WAKEFIELD lives in Federal Way, Washington. He is the author of *East of Early Winters* (University of Evansville Press, 2006) and *Robert Frost and the Opposing Lights of the Hour* (Peter Lang, 1985).

DEREK WALCOTT lives in St. Lucia, West Indies. He received

the Nobel Prize in 1992. His books include *Selected Poems* (2007), *The Prodigal* (2004), and *Omeros* (1990), all published by Farrar, Straus and Giroux.

DEBORAH WARREN lives in Andover, Massachusetts. Her books include *Dream with Flowers and Bowl of Fruit* (University of Evansville Press, 2008), *Zero Meridian* (Ivan R. Dee, 2004), and *The Size of Happiness* (Waywiser Press, 2003).

GAIL WHITE lives in Breaux Bridge, Louisiana. Her books include *Easy Marks* (David Robert Books, 2008), *Kiss and Part: Laughing at the End of Romance and Other Entanglements*, editor (Doggerel Daze Press, 2005), and *The Price of Everything* (Mellen Poetry Press, 2001).

RICHARD WILBUR lives in Cummington, Massachusetts. He twice has received the Pulitzer Prize, the first for *Things of This World: Poems* (Harcourt, Brace, 1956) and the second for *New and Collected Poems* (Harcourt Brace Jovanovich, 1988). His other books include *The Theatre of Illusion*, by Pierre Corneille (2007) and *Collected Poems, 1943-2004* (2004), both published by Harcourt.

GREG WILLIAMSON lives in Duluth, Georgia. His books include *A Most Marvelous Piece of Luck* (Waywiser Press, 2008), *Errors in the Script* (Overlook Press, 2001), and *The Silent Partner* (Story Line Press, 1995).

# About the Editor

Samuel Maio is the author of *The Burning of Los Angeles* (poems) and *Creating Another Self: Voice in Modern American Personal Poetry*, a finalist for the Christian Gauss Award. His poems have been featured in the *Los Angeles Times Book Review* and appear in several anthologies, including *California Poetry: From the Gold Rush to the Present* and *Sonnets: 150 Contemporary Sonnets*. He has received awards from the Academy of American Poets for his poetry and from Phi Kappa Phi for his literary criticism. For many years he was an associate editor of *The Formalist*, contributing essays on Hardy, Frost, Auden, Wilbur and many other modern poets. He is Professor of English and Comparative Literature at the California State University, San José, where he has served as both the Director of Creative Writing and the Director of the Center for Literary Arts. He also has taught at the University of Southern California — where he earned his Ph.D. in American literature, specializing in modern poetry — and for several years at the University of California, Davis.